DAVID BROOME'S
TRAINING MANUAL

DAVID BROOME'S
TRAINING MANUAL

MARCY PAVORD
Photographs by BOB LANGRISH

David & Charles

Thanks to the following people for their help: to the grooms big Emma, little Emma and Jenny; to Marysia; to secretaries Wendy and Sally; for typing up interview tapes to Karen and, of course, to the horses!

A DAVID & CHARLES BOOK

© Marcy Pavord 1994
First published 1994

Marcy Pavord has asserted her right to be identified as author of this work in accordance with the Copyright, Designs and Patents Act 1988.

A catalogue record for this book is available from the British Library.

ISBN 0 7153 9904 7

Typeset by ABM Typographics Ltd Hull
and printed in Italy
by Milanostampa SpA
for David & Charles
Brunel House   Newton Abbot   Devon

CONTENTS

INTRODUCTION

How does he do it?

All aspiring young show jumpers – and some maybe
not so young – believe that the answer to that one
question is the key that would unlock the door of
success. Whatever the secret is, it has worked for
David Broome for half a lifetime and kept him at the
pinnacle of what is probably the world's most popular
horse sport. And although the sport has changed –
with glittering international shows, spectacular prize
money, commercialisation and the mingled benefits
and pressures of sponsorship – the man and his
awesome talent have remained remarkably constant. From across a crowded showground, the style is
unmistakable, the quiet, rhythmic riding as uncom-
promising, as relentlessly in pursuit of excellence, as
it was in the days when David himself was inspired
by Harry Llewellyn and Pat Smythe.

David Broome is a down-to-earth, border
Welshman of the sort of farming-cum-business,
entrepreneurial stock that succeeds through dogged
determination, enlightened by clear thinking and
practical realism. Add a touch of shrewd Scottish
common sense from his mother's side, and you have
the basic qualities that have kept David's talent at
the top for so long. Fortify the mixture with a ready
sense of humour, a commitment to sportsmanship
and fair play, plus constant regard for the welfare of
his horses, and the picture is complete.

David's enthusiasm for the sport is as fresh in 1992,
the year he was selected for a record sixth Olympic
Games, as it was when he won his first Olympic
medal in Rome in 1960. Success in any sphere often
sets the star apart from his fellows, with conceit on
one side and envy on the other, but David's well
recorded popularity with colleagues throughout the
international jumping scene is a mark of his integrity
and straightforwardness. His services are much
sought in the organisation of the sport at high level,

and he is both a superb ambassador for British interests and a skilful diplomat in the political arena of show jumping.

He considers it a great honour to have followed Sir Harry Llewellyn as Chairman of the International Affairs Committee. 'He said to me the other day that there have only been two previous chairmen of that committee – Sir Michael Ansell and himself.'

His advice to the young riders who admire him is so valuable because it is honest and objective. In teaching he is kind, yet demanding; encouraging, yet direct. He believes in natural talent but also in the commitment to hard work, and he is always open to a fresh idea, or a new way of solving a problem or achieving a goal. David's own 'natural talent' is, of course, a show-jumping legend, but it took far more than that to reach and then remain at the dizzy heights of international stardom.

When he was a child, his talent was fostered and shaped by his father, Fred Broome; although this period also included a time when David was so disillusioned that he gave up riding ponies altogether. Throughout his long career, the aim has always been to win – being second best was never good enough – and today, with the immense financial strain of keeping a string of show jumpers on the road, there is still the element of whether or not the winnings from a show, large or small, will pay for the diesel for the lorry. David relates how, taking his ponies to shows as a boy, he had to work out exactly what the expenses were and whether he had won enough to be in pocket at the end of the day. That attitude, with its meticulous attention to detail, permeates David's entire philosophy towards his work; it also reflects the way the horses are treated and handled in his yard at Mount Ballan Manor, the farm near Newport, South Wales, where David has lived all his life. There is no fuss, no frenzied activity as found in many yards – instead the atmosphere is laid back, deceptively almost sleepy: but things have to be done right. There may be questions, discussions and debate, but when David makes a decision about something, it is final.

When it comes to riding, the attention to detail is

still more precise, but it is seldom explained fully in words: it is 'feel' that matters. As David says, 'You can tell people to do everything the right way, but in the end there is a "feel" about it – and if they can't feel it, it's no good.' It is, of course, the instinctive ability to get the right 'feel' that is the basis of David's tremendous success; and it is the fact that this ability is so difficult to analyse that prevents many more riders from emulating him.

The following chapters of this book describe David's methods of training horses, and riders, from novice level to Grade A, and his general horsemanship and management; it will also look at the different horses he has ridden, their individual characters and problems, and how they were directed towards success. On the way, we will try to define some of the attributes of that magical quality of 'feel'.

1 CHOOSING A SHOW JUMPER

Choosing and buying horses is a difficult business at the best of times, and nowadays, with large sums being asked for any horse with even minimal form, financially it is more risky than ever. David's advice is to be very careful, and to be sure that the horse is suited to the rider. For example there is no point in wealthy and indulgent parents paying a huge price for a horse with winning form at a high level, if their starry-eyed teenaged daughter has neither the experience nor the ability to ride at that level. The young rider will simply become frustrated, probably have her confidence undermined by her lack of success, the parents will become disillusioned and the horse will be spoilt. The need for retraining by a professional will make it difficult to sell the horse on, and impossible to recoup a decent percentage of the purchase price.

A far better option is to seek experienced advice, and to buy a horse capable of competing at a level suited to the rider's experience and ability. Ideally the horse should then progress with the rider until it reaches the limit of its potential, when it can be successfully sold on and a replacement with more scope purchased, in line with the rider's growing experience.

Finding the right horse can never be reduced to a precise art: in spite of all his experience and the many years spent buying and selling horses, even David never knows how successful a particular horse might be until it has been in his yard long enough to have its ability put to the test. Every horse is different, and although David is able to produce the best effort from each individual, that might not be enough for it to make the grade and secure a place in his team. Some may perform well at the lower levels but lack the scope, ability, soundness or temperament to progress to Grade A; others may not have the right sort of attitude and temperament to

'click' with David's particular style of riding and his very busy routine. These things are assessed during the months following a horse's arrival, and those who do not meet the necessary criteria are sold on. Frequently they remain as show jumpers, but either at a less demanding level, or with a rider who can form a more appropriate partnership. Others may go into the hunting field, or to eventing.

David is the professional: at the other end of the scale is the rider who wants to go show jumping as a hobby, rather than a career, and he is also faced with similar, if less expensive problems when looking for a suitable horse. Finally, as a last word of advice to those who take their show jumping seriously — it is important to be realistic and not persevere with a horse which has proved itself unsuitable if continual disappointment is to be avoided.

Assessing the novice show jumper. 'This young horse is jumping the oxer with plenty of "air" underneath him, and if he improves his technique with training and learns to tuck up his front legs, he will jump a considerably higher fence without needing to show any more ability.'

Finding your show jumper

So what is the least risky way to find your show-jumping horse? David returns frequently to Frank Kernan, a dealer in Ireland and the father of show jumper James Kernan, and with whom he has built up a sound relationship over the years. Frank knows the type of horse which will appeal to David, and if he rings up to suggest that he has one worth looking at, David can be confident that he won't be wasting his time and that there is a reasonable chance he will think it worth buying. Even if the horse does not become a superstar – and very few do – he knows it will at least have the potential to become a reasonable performer at basic level, and can be sold on at a fair and realistic profit.

Not everyone has direct access to a reputable specialist dealer, but buying through the personal recommendation of a friend or more experienced person who does, is still a more

'This is a horse with enormous scope, but we didn't buy him because we didn't think he would contain his jump sufficiently to cope with a whole course.'

reliable way to buy than by dipping into the classified advertisement columns of newspapers and magazines. Furthermore, if a horse proves to be unsuitable, a reputable dealer will usually come to a fair agreement for an exchange or resale, whereas there is little chance of redress against the private seller. A dealer also has his continuing good reputation to consider and is therefore more likely to sell you a horse which is actually capable of the work required.

There are plenty of unsuitable horses available, waiting for the cheque-books of the inexperienced and the unwary, so buying a horse without the necessary knowledge or without taking sensible advice, is a pitfall to avoid. If you really do not know whether a prospective purchase will suit you or not, you would be better advised to leave it and visit some shows instead, to watch and talk to the successful riders, ask their advice and perhaps arrange to have some lessons. Many successful riders also teach, as well as buy and sell horses.

David suggests that provided you don't accost them just as they are about to enter the ring, most are approachable and willing to point you in the right direction. In advising young riders, David says:

'It depends how ambitious they are and how much talent they have got, but it's important to take good advice at the start. It's like playing golf, or anything else – have a few lessons with a professional because this will start you off swinging your club the right way and getting your ideas right – there's an awful lot of ways of swinging a golf club, just as there are

of riding a horse. Natural talent is wonderful, but if you can blend it with a bit of science, all the better.'

When he has decided to buy, David insists on having the horse vetted, pointing out that if you are paying several thousands for a horse, the fee is not much extra. He always uses the same vet so that the reports he receives are consistent; veterinary reports on purchase examinations are, after all, a matter of the vet's professional opinion, which does not always reflect a cut-and-dried diagnosis. The bottom line is whether or not the vet considers the horse suitable for the purpose for which it is being purchased. David always insists on X-rays being taken of the horse's feet, to check for existing or potential problems in the bones (such as navicular disease), and as a record of the condition of the feet when the horse was purchased.

Type and conformation

Having considered how to buy a horse, the next question is, what sort of horse should you buy? David's short answer is that either it jumps, or it doesn't – although this criterion is, of course, qualified by other aspects.

Soundness is absolutely vital in a horse that is going to be trained as a show jumper, and to some extent this is covered by the precaution of vetting, as already mentioned. The horse also needs to be the right size for the prospective rider, and this not only means height, but includes its overall build, power and scope. For example a heavy, big-boned horse, standing over a lot of ground and which is hard to hold together, might need a strong rider; whereas a lighter-framed and more compact, but sensitive horse is often better ridden by a girl, regardless of its actual height.

Conformation is important, but not so important to David that he will not overlook a fault if the horse shows an ability to perform. He quotes a maxim of international rider Franke Sloothaak: 'You can forgive a horse for one fault, but you can't forgive him for two';

and sums up his own attitude to appearances thus: 'I like a horse that is pleasing to the eye; I don't like a big, ugly brute. If you were to look at all the good horses in the world, there would usually be something about them you liked; but you can have them *too* beautiful, and they're useless! I think you want to have a look at them before you see them jump, but it's only just a look – the important thing is they've got to be sharp off the floor.'

Breeding is a popular topic in the competition horse world today, but it isn't something to which David, as a competitor, has ever paid much attention. Many of his horses have originated in Ireland, a source to which he still looks today for preference, thus perhaps going against the current vogue for continental jumpers. That said, he is equally willing to consider horses from Europe or America, if they show the necessary ability. But he can explain his preference for Irish-bred horses:

'For a horse in Ireland to get to five years old he has had to use his brains to survive. He's learned to survive the chain harrows that have been abandoned, and the forty-

choosing a show jumper

gallon drum that has rusted away, and the barbed wire hanging out of the hedge. He's had to survive all that on his own – he hasn't been factory-farmed.'

So an important consideration is the horse's intelligence and ability to look after himself – a show jumper needs to be bold, but he must also be careful and a horse which has been cosseted and never exposed to danger is unlikely, later on, to know how to extricate himself from a difficult situation. Whereas a horse which has learned as a youngster to be agile and neat, and to pick his feet up out of harm's way, will have the advantage when he comes to be trained.

Although he has not personally become involved in breeding show jumpers, David does believe in breeding for performance, and thinks that any mare or stallion used for the

'This would be better if the horse was a little more relaxed; he is tucking his chin in rather than bending his neck, and needs to achieve more of a "bridge" from his nose to his tail. Riding him with more contact on the draw-reins would help.'

purpose of breeding horses for a performance career which involves jumping, should have to prove its ability to jump before being accepted for breeding. 'Unless you actually see these horses jump as three- four- and five-year-olds, they shouldn't have a licence for breeding. Nearly every horse these days has to jump at some level, be it a hunter or whatever, and if you only improved every horse's achievement by six inches, look how much safer everyone's neck would be! I think our show hunter classes are a load of rubbish; they should all be made to jump something – that is what hunting is about.'

Temperament and attitude

A horse's temperament is the link between its natural ability and its ability to learn and perform under pressure. Observing the various traits of temperament of his horses is an intrinsic part of David's constant awareness of their individual progress and problems. His acute understanding of each horse's attitude, its capacity to learn and willingness to co-operate surely plays another major part in his successfully taking so many horses to top level. Many a horse with all the right physical attributes has been rejected because its temperament and attitude could not be developed to create a sufficiently dependable partnership with the rider, thus maximising the chances of leaving the fences intact in the arena.

David gives the following blunt warning: when you go to try a horse, it is unwise to ride it yourself until you have seen someone who knows it well ride it first. 'We went to see a horse a few years ago, and when we got there the jockey was away. They asked me to ride it and I refused point blank, telling them I did not know the horse. We found out afterwards that it had not been ridden for eighteen months.

'A rough rider can ride a bad horse as well or better than I can. I don't want a fall and I don't want to be run away with, so why should I be jump jockey for someone who is not telling me the truth?'

'This is a good example of a young horse jumping a cross pole. He is arching his back nicely, not rushing, is respecting the fence and making a good shape. I know Marysia doesn't have a strong contact with his mouth, and the steeply angled cross makes the horse think and helps keep him straight.'

Some of David's horses

That there is no set pattern for a show jumping horse, in terms of both conformation and temperament, is easy to confirm by taking a look at some of the horses in David's yard. Unlike many professionals, David does not 'process' large numbers of horses through his yard. 'I don't think numbers is the answer to anything; to be truthful, numbers can ruin you. I don't want to ride five or six horses at a show – I'd rather ride three and hope it works.' Therefore all you are likely to find at any one time are two or three novices along with the Grade As, the retired horses and a strictly limited number of liveries taken in for training or assessment. For example, show jumper Marysia Orzazewska recently worked with David for a year and kept her horses stabled at Mount Ballan.

choosing a show jumper

David's novices are all purchased as his own potential future top mounts, and not for the sake of dealing; though as previously mentioned, even the most promising of purchases, with a good natural jump, can turn out to be unsuited to David's requirements and his way of doing things. Paddy, a five-year-old chestnut gelding brought over from Ireland, was one of these. In search of some novices to bring on, David was impressed by his natural ability: 'I saw him jump and he jumped very well. Then I rode him and had a nice feeling from him and I thought, well, we want to buy some novices and if we don't buy this one, we won't buy any. You don't see many that good, anyway.'

Paddy's early career was not the luckiest, however – he was dogged by a virus, and then a swelling on his girth area prevented him being worked; and he proved to be a horse who needed plenty of work. David's verdict at the time was: 'He's very arrogant, or cocky, and bucks and kicks a lot at the beginning of his work. And if he's had a long break, he doesn't start jumping until about the third class on the same day. I've never had a novice like that – you don't usually need to jump them as hard. But he's tough and he's hard, and he gets better as he keeps going. He needs the extra shots in the ring.'

Having lost time through the horse's early problems, and lacking time in the summer to school him on himself, David passed him on to Marysia, who quickly developed an understanding with him and began to enjoy some competitive success. It was clear by then that Paddy did not have the sort of calm outlook on life that would fit in with David's routine and

Paddy: 'This horse has a far more ideal conformation. He measures only just over 16hh, but proved to be very much a lady's ride, needing a very soft hand, and did not cope well with the pressure of domination by a stronger male rider.'

Showman: 'He is what I would call a good sort. He has a short front end and powerful back end, linked by a short back. Although he stands about 17hh, I would call him the "pocket battleship" type, because his size and power are concentrated into a compact package.'

busy schedule, so the decision was taken to sell him on. He found his new career show jumping abroad, and David's final comment was: 'He's a wary sort of horse, always watching things. You've got to keep on top of him to keep him doing his job, but he has a spring in him and I think, being an Irish horse, he will only get better.'

The story of Paddy illustrates clearly that it takes more than a horse with ability to form a successful show-jumping partnership with a particular rider. Horse and rider must be able to work together in tune with one another, and David would rather take the practical decision to part with a horse, than persevere with an uncomfortable partnership. However talented a particular rider or individual horse, if they are basically unsuited to each other, they will never achieve the degree of precision, co-operation and mutual trust which the sport demands at top level.

Showman is another novice, bought after David saw him jump in a four-year-old class at Millstreet Show, and is a different type of horse altogether; he has the advantage of being the type which immediately appeals to David. 'The old Irish type, he is. He's the same colour as Countryman and Sportsman, a nice peaceful sort of horse, honest and straight. He'll play you up a bit – he's not beyond being naughty – but there's a big, lazy, easy jump in him. He's a lot easier in his way than some and his graph is more consistent.'

Showman is a big, dark brown horse, standing over 17 hands high. He is substantial, with a lot of bone, yet has classy, elegant conformation which prevents him from appearing heavy. His tremendous athletic scope makes jumping easy for him – something which may not altogether be to his advantage. 'Sometimes he jumps like a big heavy lump. It's the small, easy fences that catch him out.'

Nevertheless, his career has had a promising beginning, with ample clear rounds. At one of the regular Wales and the West Shows at Mount Ballan (where there is also a permanent showground), Showman won a Gleneagles Young Horse qualifying class in his first season with David (the Gleneagles competitions were originally introduced to assess young horses on fluid jumping style and technique). 'He went absolutely beautifully, but green, and I just rode him on a nice forward stride and he just kept jumping. He was in a lovely mood that day and I could see strides from about six out, so he just kept going forward. It was obviously very pleasing to the eye.'

However, Showman's indolent temperament may also prove a drawback. David's early assessment of him was this: 'It's so easy to him, but whether he's got enough incentive to want to go . . . He's perhaps a little bit too much that way so I've got to sharpen him up. But he can be very quick, and he doesn't like to hit fences – if he hits a fence once, he won't hit it next time. He's very careful.'

A year later and Showman was still in contention; but, said David 'It's nearly make-your-mind-up time with him. He ought to be

Meynell Park: 'This horse has a rather common head, making him quite heavy in the hand. He also tends to jump rather flat, although his technique is tidy and careful.'

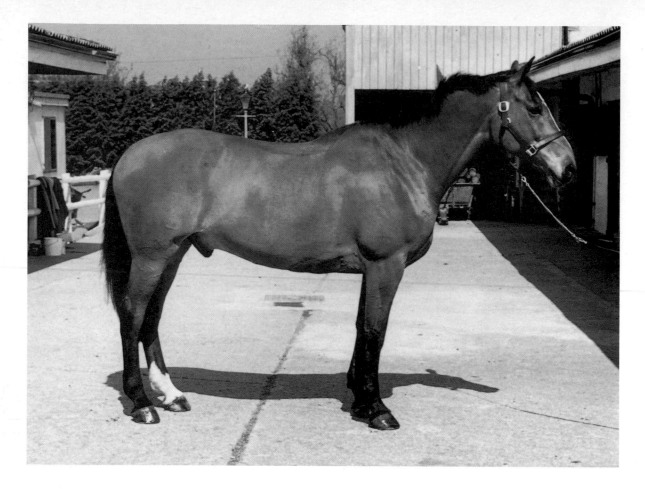

Lannegan: 'He has funny conformation, a lot higher in front than behind, whereas most show jumpers have the opposite. He's not really my type, yet he can jump! It shows what a positive mental attitude in a horse can do – how he can overcome the human impression of his shortcomings.'

ready to go on by now; he's seven, so no more excuses.' Since then, Showman has successfully made his international debut.

To replace Paddy, David acquired Meynell Park. Meynell is a solid-looking, light-bay Irish horse who gives every appearance of being placid; out hacking for exercise he is, in fact, very lazy. However, he is still prepared to spook, and he is transformed when it comes to jumping. The same age as Showman, he has begun with some competent performances at winter indoor shows – but only time will tell if he will make further improvement.

David's two top Grade As, Lannegan and Countryman, are almost mirror images of the two novices. Countryman was a member of the 1988 Olympic team at Seoul in Korea, and is a smaller version of Showman – the same

bitter chocolate colour, a classy looking, rather finely built horse with a smooth, elegant stride which would not go amiss in a three-day event dressage arena. He has a tendency – which irritates David – to stand over a lot of ground, with forelegs out in front and hindlegs stretched behind. The current star of the stable, he receives a considerable amount of fuss and attention. He displays the wisdom of the experienced horse who has been everywhere and done everything, and this in fact helps him to control his natural inclination to nervousness. He is touchy, ticklish and sensitive, trembling at loud noises or implied threats. For example he delighted head girl Emma Storey by allowing her to clip his face for the first time – then promptly blotted his copybook by lashing out and catching her on the knee. An X-ray and some heavy bandaging later, Emma bore the superstar not the least grudge.

Despite his successes, Countryman still has his problems: 'When John [Whitaker] beat him in the King George, Countryman

had dropped into a trot on a very tight corner in the jump-off,' David recalls ruefully. 'Otherwise we may have beaten him.'

Lannegan, just as successful and actually more consistent than his stablemate, is nicknamed Lofty. A light and striking bay with a white blaze, he has the sort of physical build that makes successful training difficult, and David admits that he almost rejected him on his conformation. He has an enormous front with a high wither, and this runs into a long back and flat croup, and what David refers to as 'an awful back end'. So why didn't David reject him?

'He always had a jump and he was always careful, although ungainly.' And Emma adds to the picture: 'He's lovely – he always wants to win for you.'

Lannegan's awkward physical attributes mean that he takes a long time to warm up and, with his extremely long stride, is not easy to hold together. Interestingly, David notes that 'Countryman and Lannegan are very different. I rarely ride them both in the

Feedback: 'A good continental warmblood type, slightly flat-backed, but on the whole a good sort who has proved his worth over the years.'

same class and if one is going well, the other usually isn't.'

The third Grade A in David's current top string is the less renowned, but nevertheless successful chestnut Feedback. A contemporary of Countryman and Lannegan, David acknowledges that when the three first came to him, he would have considered Feedback to have had the greatest potential. Feedback is also the odd one out from a breeding point of view, being a continental-bred horse of German and Dutch origin.

Finally, David does not forget past successes. Many riders pay only lip-service to the 'happy retirement' of old campaigners, but David's former stars have a proper and caring home at Mount Ballan. The senior incumbent nowadays is the great Philco, who shares his field and sometimes his stable with a pony companion.

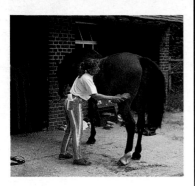

2
CARE AND MANAGEMENT

For a new horse arriving at the yard there is a reassuring air of calm, and most settle down quickly to a straightforward routine. New arrivals are stabled for the first few days and kept separate from the other horses, particularly the Grade A jumpers, who are always kept in their own separate boxes to minimise the risk of any infection or virus being passed to them from other inmates. All the horses are routinely vaccinated against equine influenza. The newcomer will be given a basic diet of 'chop' (molassed chaff), plus a few competition nuts and hay, until his temperament and individual requirements become apparent. At first he will be worked very quietly, hacking out with a steady companion while the staff get to know him, and also to be sure that he is traffic proof, since exercising in the immediate vicinity of the yard involves coping with several busy main roads.

The novice horses are usually brought into work during the winter and will be rugged up, clipped and have their manes and tails pulled to tidy them up for the indoor shows.

The working yard

The Broome showjumping yard is tidy and well ordered, but not aggressively so. Set in the midst of a working farm, the atmosphere is one of workmanlike practicality rather than the militaristic 'spit and polish' régime so often found in top equestrian establishments. The grounds are neat, the grass mown, the yard well swept, but there has been no 'prettifying' with hanging baskets and flower tubs. The attitude is one of total involvement with the job in hand – training show jumpers – with no time for non-essential gloss.

Two neat rows of block-built, whitewashed boxes face each other across a wide, concreted, open walkway. They are light, airy and with high ceilings, admitting plenty of fresh air: David is highly conscious of the fact that show jumpers are most susceptible to re-

spiratory diseases, resulting from the amount of time they spend cooped up in confined spaces, both when travelling and in the often less-than-ideal accommodation provided at many shows. Each box has a built-in concrete manger with a hay rack over, so that spilt hay falls into the manger and not on the floor. All are fitted with automatic drinking bowls. The lower half-doors are relatively high, and more suited to taller horses; but then most of the occupants stand at least 16.2hh.

Near the entrance and close to the house is the feed room, where hard feed is stored hygienically in galvanised bins. The hay barn is some distance away – again, mindful of the dangers of dust and spores – and the hay and HorseHage are brought up by barrow as required. Adjoining the feed room is a washing-down room, with hot and cold water laid on and a concrete floor sloping to a drain, where the horses are prepared for shows. Manes and

The yard at Mount Ballan: head girl Emma Storey with guard dog 'Boss' and a student ready to ride out.

tails are pulled, not plaited, although the day before a show, manes are divided into bunches and plaited loosely to encourage them to lie flat. Outside, steps lead up to the staff flat, from the tool and barrow store.

Backing on to the opposite row of boxes is the large indoor school – actually a farm storage building and often piled with straw bales and other produce – where most of the basic flatwork and training is done. Built about thirty years ago, the riding surface is simply topsoil and it still serves its purpose well. Practice jumps, some of them home-made, are stacked in the centre, ready to be brought out to build grids and practice fences.

Beyond are more stables, and down a slope, the farm buildings and the permanent show-rings of the Wales and the West Showground. Surprisingly, David avoids using most of these extensive facilities for training, the main rings being reserved for use on show days only.

Feeding

The day starts at 7am when head girl Emma Storey sees to the early feeding. The horses' diets are based on good forage. 'We make a lot of HorseHage on the farm and we feed it to the horses. We buy in our hay, because all our good grass goes into making the HorseHage,' David explains. 'We deal with a local man who keeps us right for our oats, and we grind them ourselves. In the winter we also feed a little bit of boiled barley and sugar beet, but we try not to overdo the hard feed.'

David's tried and tested principles follow the theory that is increasingly taking over from the traditional high concentrate, low forage methods of feeding hunters and racehorses: that horses perform better on a good quality, high fibre diet, supplemented with concentrates for energy only as required. 'There's no point in putting feed into horses if you then have to take it out of them with extra work,' David points out. 'It can cost you a lot of money to give yourself a lot of work! We try to keep the horses in nice condition and you want them reasonably hard and fit, but there is no point in overfuelling the fire, so we restrict the high protein and more or less stick to straights.

'It's a question of getting the balance right, really. We went down the road where it cost us an absolute fortune trying bits of this and bits of that, but additives are the highest profit-making products that feed merchants can sell. You've got to use your brains a little bit – and in the end they either jump or they don't jump, and we've come back to old-fashioned straight feeding.'

The HorseHage which David manufactur-ers and uses, is a form of ensiled hay and is dust-free, so is particularly useful for horses with allergic respiratory conditions; it also helps to minimise the incidence of such dis-eases, given the inevitably high-risk lifestyle of the show-jumping horse. Packed and sealed in plastic-covered bales, it is cleaner and easier to transport to shows than bales of hay. It has the advantage of being palatable and enjoyed by most horses, and since it possesses a higher nutritional value than hay, it also reduces the quantity of concentrates required.

DATE	HORSE	TREATMENT	LUNCH
	JIMMY	1 B 1 O ½ CM ½ N	CM
	PHILCO	1 B 1 MF 1 CM ½ N	CM
	DENNIS	1 B 1 MF ½ CM ½ N CHOP	N
	PATRICK	1 B 1 O ½ CM ½ N	CM
	WHISPER	1 B ½ MF ½ N CHOP	N
	MENNELL	1 B 1 O ½ CM ½ N	CM
	JOEY	½ B DENGIE ½ N	
	FLICKER	HAY NO FOOD VERY FAT	N
	LOFTY	1 B 1 O ½ CM ½ N	CM
	WIZZ	½ B DENGIE ½ N	
	DAISY	1 B ½ O ½ CM ½ MF ½ N CHOP	N
	DIGGER	1 B ½ O ½ CM ½ MF ½ N CHOP	N

The horses' rations, down to the smallest pony 'Flicker', are listed on the feed room blackboard under their stable names.

'Now whose is this . . .?' Emma mixes the feeds from the galvanised storage bins, which keep the food clean and discourage mice.

A major problem in feeding top class competition horses is the need to be sure that feeds are not contaminated with any substance included in the FEI (Fédération Équestre Internationale) prohibited substances list, because these horses may be dope tested at any time; so when feeding compounds such as cubes and coarse mixes, it is essential to buy only those which carry the appropriate manufacturer's guarantee. Straights must also come from an uncontaminated source.

Among the permissible additives which Emma does use are garlic – long acknowledged as a valuable tonic – and a mixed herb supplement designed especially for horses, a useful source of essential nutrients for animals which spend much of the time stabled, and do not have the opportunity for the selective grazing which is natural to the horse kept outdoors.

It is not only foodstuffs which need to be monitored, since horses can also absorb substances through the skin. Shampoos and washes, fly repellents, and all ointments and embrocations such as wound dressings and cooling gels, must also be free of prohibited substances, or their use avoided until after the competition.

The horses are fed three times a day – first thing in the morning, again at lunchtime, and at about 5pm. Quantities are kept relatively low, with a couple of pounds of concentrates usually being the maximum given for any one feed. Each horse's diet, with the quantities required for each feed, is chalked up on a list in the feed room, thus ensuring that all the horses receive their individual requirements and that a check is kept on what they eat. David emphasises the need to treat horses as individuals, although he admits that he is less of an expert when it comes to feeding than was his father.

'He was brilliant at it – he studied every one down to the smallest detail. To some extent he'd be horrified now at the way we feed, compared to how he used to do it. He would know, down to a quarter scoop of corn, how much was needed for the accelerator. He used to feed my ponies and he was the one who used to have the sleepless night before a show, not me!'

Dentistry

To obtain maximum nutritional benefit from his food a horse must be able to chew it properly, and like many top professionals, David calls upon a specialist horse dentist rather than his vet to care for his horses' teeth. The horse dentist visits the yard about twice a year and will spend a whole day checking all the horses' mouths, rasping off the sharp edges that inevitably occur on the outer edge of the upper molars and inner edge of the lower molars, and also dealing with any other specific problems. The horse dentist will often work in conjunction with the vet if, for example, a horse needs to be sedated for his dentistry treatment.

The dentist's work is also important when it comes to the horse feeling comfortable with the bit. If his mouth is sore due to a problem with his teeth, he will not be able to accept the bit and work properly. 'If the mouth is wrong, you'll get nothing out of the horse,' says David.

Basic stable management

The standard bedding for David's horses is woodshavings. 'They're expensive – it costs about £10 or £11 to make a horse bed – but it's a lot easier for mucking out and the bales we use have a lot of the dust taken out.'

Dust is a major hazard in the lives of show-jumping horses since they spend so much time travelling and stabled, not only in their own boxes but also in show stables; these often have ventilation that is less than satisfactory, which certainly contributes to the risk of respiratory problems. Show jumpers may only be in the ring and performing for a short time, but . . . 'They still work pretty hard. You get fourteen efforts in fifty-five seconds – it's at least a jump every four seconds or so – and for that they've got to have a quick supply of oxygen.

'You walk into a lot of the show stables we're in and the bad air hits you, wallop! But a lot of people don't take any notice.

'We do sometimes use paper bedding if a horse has an allergy.'

At home the horses are given a quick groom, or quartering, before work and a thorough rub-down afterwards. They work hard, and are kept both muscled up and well covered, giving the lie to another fallacy – that show jumpers don't need to be fit. In fact those competitors whose horses are well covered but are soft, will not find success in the show-jumping ring. The show jumper often has continental warmblood or Irish blood in his make-up and is usually a more heavily built animal than the event horse or, certainly, the racehorse; but the fact that he doesn't have a Thoroughbred's 'greyhound' type physique does *not* mean he can get away with being fat. Although top jumping horses may not appear lean, they will have well developed and powerful muscles which, together with joints, tendons, ligaments and bones, need a considerable amount of the right kind of work if they are to develop to their full capacity of fitness and power.

If David's horses are away at shows, however, they are groomed thoroughly three times a day to get rid of dust, sweat and travel stains and to keep their coats gleaming and healthy.

In winter the working horses are clipped right out, and the clip is redone regularly. To compensate for the loss of protection against the cold normally provided by their winter coats, they are warmly rugged, with several light layers rather than one heavy one. The rugs are checked several times a day and changed frequently to avoid any risk of rubbing or pressure sores. Nevertheless some top show jumpers are no more co-operative

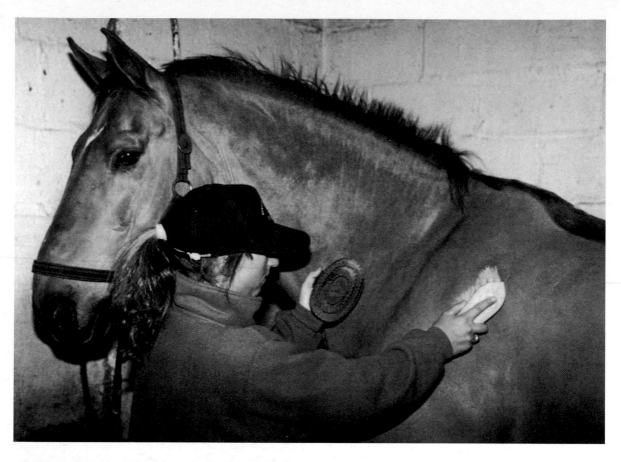

Feet are always picked out just before the horse goes out of his stable, to avoid dropping bedding in the yard.

Emma's Swedish dandy brush is one of her favourite grooming tools. Feedback gets a tidy-up before work.

than the average horse when it comes to making rugs last: 'Lofty eats his,' says Emma ruefully; nor has she come up with a practical deterrent.

Clipping continues until around mid-April, when the summer coat starts to come through.

Traditional 'strapping', vigorous grooming of the large muscle areas using a wisp made of plaited hay, is not done as often as it used to be, reflects David. 'But you can get a horse half fit with proper strapping and we ought to do a lot more of it than we do.'

The groom's duties

A glimpse behind the scenes in a top show-jumping yard is a fascinating experience. The golden rule is that the horses always come first, and a good show-jumping groom must be prepared to work hard and always remember that, whether getting up at 3 o'clock in the

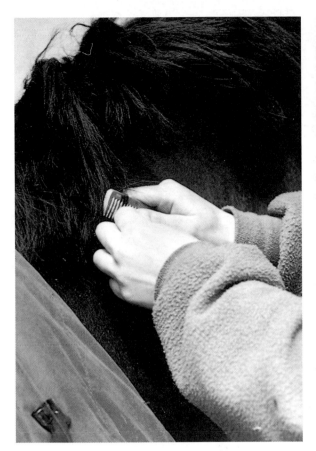

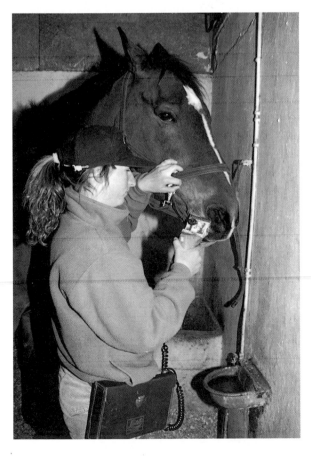

Showman's mane and tail are pulled to a tidy and manageable length.

morning to prepare horses to travel to a show, or waiting for the last jumping class to finish at 11 o'clock at night before driving the horses home and putting them comfortably to bed. This is no nine to five job!

Apart from the daily routine, the head girl has the added responsibilities of running the yard – booking farrier and vet appointments, getting running repairs done to tack and equipment, keeping the lorry in order and keeping up stocks of feed and bedding, to name just a few jobs.

Regular clipping is part of the routine and the clippers with portable power pack are an essential part of Emma's equipment. Here she gives Lannegan's muzzle a trim.

The daily work routine

The working day's routine varies according to the time of year and what needs to be done. There may be a young rider who has brought horses to David for lessons, in which case the training will be intensive and hard work, so that both student and horses learn and are improved as much as possible in the short time available.

David's own horses and any others in the yard such as liveries in for training, will be worked or ridden out according to their individual programmes. A horse recovering from injury, or those who have just been brought in from grass, may go out on walking exercise; if a horse is suspected of being 'not quite right' it might be lunged so that David can pinpoint the problem. He might decide to ride a particular horse to try and solve a difficulty that has cropped up in the arena, or he and Marysia might work together, bringing on novices or liveries.

The Grade A jumpers are usually worked in the school or ridden out by Emma. It might surprise many people that David allows anyone else to ride such valuable top performers, but his commitments often take him away from home for several days, even if he is going to a show, some horses will be left behind. 'David has taught me the way he wants the horses ridden,' says Emma; and so even if days pass when David himself cannot ride, he

Walking exercise is essential when the horses first come into work after their break, or for a new horse just starting out. Emma Storey is exercising Showman – wearing knee boots as a young horse out on the road should – while Emma Lipscomb rides Feedback.

knows that Countryman, Lannegan and Feedback are getting the work they need, in the way that he wants.

Young and novice horses are not worked every day. 'I don't think they want too much, especially a five- or six-year-old,' David explains. 'You want to keep it pleasant and enjoyable for them, and if you overwork them too often they are going to get mentally sick of it, aren't they?'

 David says: 'Feedback is "taking Emma for a ride", and Emma's mind is elsewhere! A sneaky shot, catching them unawares, with neither horse nor rider concentrating!'

'Sometimes we load them in the lorry and go up to Wentwood. We go for an hour-and-a-half's ride over the hills, let them pick their way up, things like that. I might take them on a local 'fun ride', just popping over the fences in the wood, more or less the same as you do out hunting, and that's quite enjoyable.'

A hunting education

David is also a Master of the local hunt, the Curre. 'It's a good little hunt, stuck in the backwoods of beyond, but we do our own little thing. Most of the novices see hounds. Being Master I can pick my own spots, which is very useful. I think it's nice if they can wander through a wood picking their own way and watching where they put their feet, maybe go through a stream and watch out for the odd ditch, and just generally become aware of things. Of course, you've got to be careful you

don't get trapped in a place where you end up galloping down a road – my horses are too expensive for that! I always hunt for my horse's sake, not for the cheeky fellow!

'It all helps them to use their heads and brains and jump things. They've got to learn to think, haven't they?'

This type of exercise is geared towards educating and settling the horse down and developing his mental attitude to his work, and to strengthening and fittening his body.

Fittening work

At the start of the competition year, horses which have been out at grass – even older ones – will be given six weeks walking exercise when they come back in before being asked to do anything more strenuous. This is to give the bones, tendons and ligaments of the limbs and joints a chance to strengthen

without stress, thus minimising the risk of the show-jumping horse's most frequent problem, stress-related injury. A horse with even the best possible conformation will still be prone to injury if his training is not carefully monitored on a progressively increasing scale. An unfit horse cannot balance himself or carry his rider correctly, and if asked to do too much, will be more likely to suffer injury; this could be anything from a minor overreach to a major disaster such as a ruptured

The benefits of taking a young horse out hunting: he receives about five hours consecutive work, and a good education.

care and management

tendon. Continual overwork will result in trouble in the joints, with eventual bone problems and arthritis. For a professional show jumper like David, a horse out of action for any length of time is not earning its keep and is an expense he would rather not have to afford; so particular attention is paid to progressive work, and a horse is only asked to perform when he is ready for the task.

The same theory is applied even more rigorously to the horse's daily exercise. Horses which are to be worked in the school are always given a carefully graduated warming-up period, often being walked out first. In the school they are worked for an hour or sometimes more, but in a progressive way, beginning with walking exercises, progressing to trot and finally to canter, with a strong emphasis on suppling exercises such as circles, changes of rein and shoulder-in. The level of concentration and performance required on the flat is always commensurate with the horse's stage of training. At the end of the session a cooling down period is equally important; the horse will usually be taken for a short walk outside to cool down and relax, before he is untacked and put back in his stable for grooming.

The importance of shoeing

The athletic effort of landing over big fences puts tremendous stress not only on the horse's forelegs, but on his feet. The foot looks simple enough from the exterior, but is of course a very complicated part of the anatomy. The insensitive outer areas of the hoof wall, sole and frog must be correctly cared for by the farrier to minimise the risk of damage to the sensitive internal structures – laminae, bones, cartilages and tendons – and to keep them working well mechanically and sound.

David's farrier visits his yard regularly once a week, to keep the horses' feet in good order. In the past David has tried various experimental horseshoes, but has settled for the ordinary fullered hunter shoe, unless an individual horse has any special need for corrective shoeing. For jumping, studs are often required for the temporary period of the competition; however, they seriously unbalance the horse's feet so must be removed as soon as the competition is over. Shoes must be fitted with special holes into which the studs are screwed, and there are various types to suit differing ground conditions.

'We nearly always use studs outside, even if the ground is firm. We use the little short sharp ones unless it's wet, when we use a deeper one – working on the principle that if they don't do much good, they don't do much harm either, and there are times when they are very important. We sometimes put two in each front shoe, but always a small one on the inside, in case the horse catches himself. On the back we use a bigger stud. We rarely use studs indoors, though a lot of people do.'

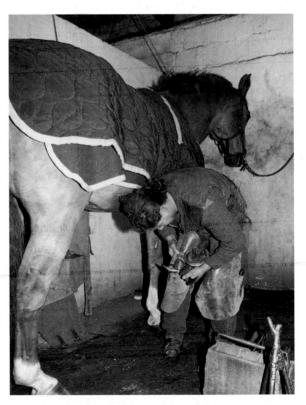

Correctly balanced feet and good shoeing are essential. The farrier visits regularly, once a week.

3
THE NOVICE HORSE: FLATWORK

David is in the school, watching Marysia ride a new horse, a five-year-old chestnut mare bought in Ireland a few weeks previously, named Two To Tango. She was shipped home and has been in work at David's yard for about a fortnight. So what does he think of the mare and her prospects?

'We saw this jump at Millstreet and it was very green, but it did throw a couple of jumps. It's a bit of a gamble really – it could finish up as anything. It could be quite good, or it could be totally normal.' There is a pause, then he deigns to acknowledge the mare with her gender.

'She was genuine, with a nice attitude. She's not a bad sort, though I hate chestnut mares – I couldn't believe I'd actually bought one! – but in fact she's not the worst I've known.'

That is about the best that David will say about the horse at this stage, even though he admits the mare's conformation is basically good, and she trots round calmly with a relaxed and happy attitude. There is nothing he particularly likes or dislikes about her. 'She is what she is – you make the best of what you've got.'

Again he quotes Franke Sloothaak: 'You can excuse a horse for one fault; you can't excuse it for two.' This is a maxim to which David continually returns when summing up equine ability. 'It's quite true. If a horse is perfect in every way, with a perfect mouth but, say, a little bit untidy in front, you can improve the untidiness in its jump. If it's a bit scatty but has a good mouth you can ride it – but if it's scatty with a bad mouth, you've got problems.'

Assessing the potential jumper

Assessing the way a new horse goes will give David a good idea of its future potential, and there are both positive and negative aspects to this. What are the characteristics to be avoided?

'I hate a horse that puts his tongue over the bit – that's awful; or one that keeps changing his back legs and gets disunited all the time. And you don't want his head either stuck in the clouds or stuck to his chest. I like a horse that basically wants to please you, not a nappy or hot-headed one.'

On the positive side, David looks for horses that track up well. 'The back end should be right underneath a horse's body – a horse that can't track up well is a hard one to ride, because his back end is always behind him. Nor does he want to be too heavy in your hand – and the lighter he touches the floor the better. It should be just a tap, you should never hear them on the floor. You never hear Countryman on the floor. Phil Harris [David's long-time sponsor and friend] always said you should hardly be able to hear them, the good ones, and it's true.' David compares this ideal to a visiting horse he doesn't like: 'He's heavy on the floor, you can hear him coming down the school.'

Action also plays a part in the assessment. 'There have been very few daisy cutters that have been good show jumpers. Most of them have a little bit of height in the action somewhere.' Another horse is described as 'a slippery eel – I just wouldn't be interested in it. Its feet go off at all angles. The good ones have to help you, be positive in their outlook on life and they have to be light on the floor.'

The importance of assessing a horse right at the start of its career becomes evident when David talks about the purpose of training, and it highlights the difficulty that has to be faced when someone comes along with a horse which they love and cherish, but which David knows will never make the top. In these cases David will do the best he can for the horse – as he will with all horses whose owners ask him for help – whilst giving the owner an honest assessment, yet trying not to deflate too many hopes and dreams. 'If someone's got a dream, who am I to stop them?'

But anyone hoping to make a show jumper out of any young horse would be wise to assess it in David's terms, and to take heed of his fundamental beliefs about training. 'If it was a question of training and *only* a question of training we'd all have superstars, and six to ten of them; but the training only helps those with natural talent. It can polish the corners of the talent, but it can't make it, and the good one is born a good one. With all the training in the world you can't make another Milton, until another Milton comes along. I've had some smashing horses, but they had that jump in them from day one – a raw, green jump, but they had that ability.'

So much for the theory that horses are not natural jumpers. They may not jump through choice at liberty or in the wild, but to make a show jumper, a horse must be willing to try when asked, then training can refine the raw material to the high standard of performance required to cope with jumping a number of testing obstacles cleanly in a relatively confined space. And during the training process even the best horse will encounter problems:

'There will be setbacks during his career that you will have to overcome, and you must be able to see them happening. I remember once, with Heatwave, I won a class at the Royal Highland and in my enthusiasm against the clock I galloped him over two fences. I was awake till three o'clock that night thinking I could have ruined him.' David shakes his head in disbelief at the memory. 'I galloped him! As it was, he went a bit quick the next day but I got him back, and that was all right.

'Then with Sportsman in 1972, his first Nations Cup was Dublin and it was the biggest course in Europe that year. He actually went round for two four-faulters – it was two rounds. One horse beat him and that was Simona (the good German mare), but it nearly ruined Sportsman – he didn't win a class for twelve months after that. He would panic. Those oxers were so big in this class, that even though we hadn't over-jumped him as a young horse, these over-faced him. He didn't forget and he didn't forgive me, and I had to ride him quietly for a year to get him to settle in his mind again about the jumps, because I had scared him to death. He had seventeen seconds before he won another class, and he wasn't the same horse for ages.

'So, these are the sort of things you can do, and you can ruin horses so easily. Some people have the reputation of ruining a horse in two weeks – they just have that way of going about things.'

With David's preference for Irish horses, what sort of 'natural ability' does he look for, when he goes over to buy? 'No matter how the horse is riding, it should be able to hack round at 4ft and pop it; it should show a bit of courage.'

Hunting: an education

The good-looking bay horse, Showman, was a typical Irish purchase, although only just backed and jumping a pole when he came to his new home. To further his education and broaden his outlook David took him hunting: 'I hunted him quite a number of times, for just an hour-and-a-half or two hours, but without hunting hard. He would trot round and enjoy himself and look at the hounds and just look at life really.'

David is a firm believer in hunting as a means of teaching young horses to concentrate and look after themselves. 'It's a wonderful thing, because you get into different places and circumstances and you're riding for several hours at a time which you wouldn't normally do, but you're not drilling them. It's all happening naturally. They've got banks to negotiate, trees to go round, cattle and sheep to go past, hounds running in and out of their legs, other horses bumping into them, and it's all happening. I think it's great for them, as long as they don't get kicked and you don't abuse them.'

Every horse, whether a young novice starting serious work for the first time, or an older horse who has had a lay-off, needs some preparatory work before going into the indoor school to start what David calls 'drilling'. They are ridden out for at least a month, just walking at first, then quietly building up to a little trotting. 'It gives them a chance for their muscles to get used to work. Ideally they should have eight weeks of this, but for the last two or three weeks you would start to work them as well.'

Initial groundwork

Even when 'real' work begins the approach is still relaxed, with the aim of seeing how the horse reacts and responds and how well balanced it is naturally, before any more pressurised work is imposed. The chestnut mare, Two To Tango, is trotted around the school and it becomes apparent that today she is finding it difficult to turn to the left. However, it is not a major problem and no one gets very worried about it; perhaps she is just a little stiff from the unaccustomed work of the previous few days. She is given some warming-up exercises at trot and canter consisting of circles and changes of rein, and the left rein improves. In order to continue improving the left bend she is then given a few jumps over a single fence placed across the school, on a circle to the left.

The following week she went to her first indoor show with Marysia, and although David was not impressed with her style – it did not show the same ability as on the day she had attracted his notice in Ireland – she won her class.

With a new horse, the first lesson is mainly one of finding the horse's attitude and level of ability. 'You trot him round, and usually find he trots one way better than the other. Then you begin with circles and simple things like this, just to keep him supple and keep his mind contented. There is no point in doing high pressure work like figures-of-eight too soon – horses can't take it mentally. So you keep it simple and try to get them balanced and in a nice shape.

'Milton has been a lovely balanced horse all his life apparently. Not many are like that, but with practice and repetition you try to influence a horse so that it develops a nice, natural cadence, which you can work from to help it jump.'

As the horse improves, other work is intro-duced. 'You start with circles and squares, then eventually you proceed to figures-of-eight, shoulder-in, a little bit of half-pass and finally you try to make them extend the stride in trot, in a straight line. Then you probably fit all this in with a little jumping – a few crosses and simple fences, and keep the whole thing interesting.'

David is particularly careful not to ask too much of a horse at this early stage of its career. There is no set length of time for a lesson, nor does he insist on achieving a particular goal each time. 'They don't need an hour's drilling every day of the week, because mentally they couldn't handle it and training shouldn't be like that. You should vary their work and make it interesting for them. When they are young, five or eight minutes of one exercise is plenty, even if you are not really succeeding; you should abandon it to the next day or the day after, then have another chip at it.'

 # Breeding and temperament

'They do vary as to how much work you can give them, depending on what breed they are. A five-year-old Warmblood is a lot more mentally and physically developed than an Irish horse of the same age. The Irish horse will keep on developing until he's twelve years old, but the Warmblood will probably be nearly as good at five years old as he will be at twelve, so he can stand a bit more work at an earlier stage. When you try an Irish horse, if he jumps 4ft or 4ft 3in pretty well, you know that when he's ten he'll have developed along the right lines. The Warmblood really wants to show you what he can do at five years old, because he's not going to develop a lot more.'

There are few Thoroughbreds at the top in show jumping, but David observes: 'Of course American history has been made on the Thoroughbred, show-jumping-wise. They are different again and about halfway between the Irish and the Warmblood. They are probably quicker than the Irish and yet they can develop their jump more as the years go on.'

One of the keys to David's success is to treat all horses, both his own and those that come to him for training, as individuals. There is no set formula or pattern of work that can be packaged as a system or method, and perhaps that is one of the reasons why trying to analyse David's skill is so difficult. Even the earliest training will vary, as what one horse needs will not necessarily be best for another character.

In Britain, little has been done to keep breeding records of show-jumping horses, but on the continent, breeding policies specifically for the sport are beginning to bear fruit and the new British Horse Database should go a long way towards helping produce British-bred jumping horses in the future.

However, no breeding policy can produce horses to order or to operate with machine-like precision and David's ability to recognise an individual animal's needs and be flexible in his training methods is a major aspect of his skill.

Long-reining

When David is working with a young horse from the floor, he prefers long-reining to lungeing. 'I think driving is quite good for them – they've got to come around you and you can teach them to canter round and work to a circle. I think lungeing is more useful later on, when they accept everything else and do everything naturally for you.' For long-reining, the horse is fitted with a snaffle

 'I go through phases of using long-reining, and I really prefer using two reins to the single lunge rein because it gives you much more flexibility and control.'

bridle and a saddle, with the stirrups tied together with a strap under the girth to prevent them flapping. The reins are passed from the bit through the stirrup irons and back to the handler.

Lungeing and 'gadgets'

Horses may be lunged for several reasons: to encourage a novice to move in a better outline, to warm up an older horse coming back into work, or to exercise one who is not being ridden for some reason; and David frequently uses a Chambon. This simple piece of equipment is named after the French cavalry officer who invented it, and consists of a strap attached to the girth which then divides at the chest into two lengths of cord; these pass up and through rings attached to a headpiece on

either side of the poll, down alongside the cheekpieces of the bridle and are then clipped to the bit. The Chambon prevents a horse from raising his head above a certain level, depending how tightly it is fitted: thus when he lowers his head to the required degree, the pressure of the Chambon on the poll and corners of the mouth relaxes. He can then be lunged on the circle, and in effect is encouraged to lift his back and bring his hind legs further underneath his body, thus engaging

🏇 'I have no great preference for either the Chambon or de Gogue. The basic purpose again is to have the horse making the "bridge" from nose to tail. Some horses work better in one, some in the other, and some in neither.'

the power in his hindquarters, which is needed for the explosive effort of jumping.

The Chambon must be fitted loosely at first to give the horse the opportunity to get used to the restriction. Most horses soon learn to accept it, David says, though some will go against it. 'Most soon cotton on that if they soften up, instead of stiffening against the bit, it doesn't hurt any more, so it is in their own interests to "give" to it.' The Chambon is used for both young and older horses. 'I use it when I think they're going the "wrong way up" – I've even warmed up Countryman in one for a

🏇 Showman working in the de Gogue. 'Here he is resisting, as shown by the tightness of the lungeing rein and the martingale.'

competition; very often, with these little things, you change them around when the notion takes you. It's very important to be flexible about what you do.'

The same guidelines apply to the use of all so-called 'gadgets'. 'It depends why a horse is doing what he's doing,' David explains. 'And you've got to get the horse to "give" a bit before you start putting a new attachment on it, because if it suddenly freaked out, it could do itself a lot of damage. They don't usually go bananas if, for example, you put on a standing martingale – it doesn't hurt and it keeps them in basically the right shape. What we're trying to do, I suppose, is to dictate, or influence the shape of the horse, and we all have our own ideas and do it a little bit differently.'

The purpose of training on the flat

How does David describe the 'shape' he is seeking?

'We are trying to make a bridge from the nose to the tail, including the back and everything else – it's very difficult to shorten a horse when his back is dipped, as his conformation is working against you.'

As most of the horses coming to the yard are already broken in and have started a little jumping, very little basic training is done from the floor. The whole training process is aimed at improving the horse's capability to jump, and initially this means improving suppleness, muscular development and obedience. Lessons commence in a relaxed, easy way: 'I'll get on the horse, walk it round, then trot it in a nice easy manner in rising trot. Then I'll start to bring it in a little bit by shortening its stride and trotting on a circle in both directions.

'If the horse is going nicely and is balanced, I'll go on and do a little shoulder-in and half-pass. Then I'll do the same thing all over again at the canter.'

So far as the young horse is concerned, shoulder-in and half-pass are learned progressively. 'At first you just try to make the horse move away from the leg – you're certainly not going to get perfection at that age, but, as time goes by it will get better and better. We do most of the dressage movements – we'd probably only get two out of ten for them in a dressage test, but we do them!

Basically the idea is to get all the "hinges" or joints moving; they have to move when you're going over a jump, but if you've got areas of the body which are blocked off in flatwork, they are going to be blocked off in jumping. Then you can't lengthen and shorten the

Showman in shoulder-in: 'Mentally, Showman accepts flatwork exercises better than many horses. I've known naturally balanced horses who wouldn't do any work at home, but most horses need this type of work and it helps if the horse is willing to co-operate.'

Showman in half-pass: 'From a dressage point of view I'd probably get one out of ten, but it serves my purpose in making the horse obedient and supple.'

stride, and you can't do all those little extra things that hopefully make the horse very athletic and free at the jump.

'Shoulder-in, for example, gets the horse's hocks up underneath him. A show jumper really has to get his hind legs up underneath him, so it's a very good exercise.

'The half-pass is a question of making the horse move away from your legs – and it doesn't do any harm to broaden the young horse's horizons a bit! With a novice I might start in walk, and you can do these exercises along the wall of the school, or you can point him straight at the wall to help teach him to move sideways.'

One of David's favourite schooling exercises is a small figure-eight, performed at the trot at one end of the school along the short side. 'It's a great way of settling a buzzy one; give it five minutes of that and it will begin to settle down. You keep turning back into the wall, so the horse can't wander out; use the corners of the school or a hedge of some sort to help you.

'I also often do it to make sure a horse is sound, because if there is any lameness the figure-eight will find it out straightaway.'

David also points out that most people, when schooling, tend always to ride along the outside track of the school so that the wall supports the horse. 'Another useful exercise, when you are cantering around, is to go two metres out from the side and try to keep the horse moving in a straight line. You will find it's difficult to do!'

Of course in the show-jumping arena the horse performs at canter, and David's young horses are introduced to canter work almost immediately, with all the exercises progressively introduced, starting with large circles. David draws from his fund of analogies to explain the relationship between rider and horse, and what the rider is trying to achieve: 'When you ride a horse, you are trying to instruct it without it being able to see you. It's like standing behind a Japanese man who doesn't understand any English, and giving him instructions how to get somewhere. Everything you try to teach a horse, it does naturally by itself; it stops and it turns left and right, so why should it be awkward when you want it to do it for you? You have to create a language in which you can both communicate.'

The same basic approach to flatwork is used with all the horses, whatever the stage of their careers, with much the same exercises employed. Changing the leading leg at the canter, for example, is developed naturally as part of the canter work and is essential for quick changes of direction in the arena. 'But you wouldn't let a Grade A show jumper get away with the same level of work as a novice. I can get horses to change leads on every other stride without too much trouble. Manhattan could change on every stride.'

The other vital requirement is for horses to be able to lengthen and shorten strides in their approach to a jump. 'That is the ultimate aim, to be able to lengthen a stride then shorten it. But they have to be able to do everything else before you can teach them that.'

Riding in draw-reins

The one schooling aid which David – in common with most show-jumping riders – uses almost as a matter of course with every horse is the so-often criticised draw-rein. In fact top show jumpers are frequently the butt of criticism for using this, and other gadgets, which would appear to have little or no place in the general good training of the riding horse. In the case of draw-reins the criticism is no doubt partially justified, in that incorrectly used, they may well result in an overbent horse which is not using its hindquarters properly. However, for any piece of equipment to be effective, the user must know the right way to use it, and this applies no less to draw-reins than any other artificial aid.

Why does David put them on almost every horse for schooling? 'You don't have to *over-use* them – all you are asking is for the horse to flex to them and stay supple. I use them only on a snaffle bridle, unless there's some particular reason for using another bit; but if I'm going out to work a horse, it will usually be in a snaffle bridle.

'Riding with a draw-rein is a great art, but I think I've been lucky enough to witness one or two people who have been supreme artists at using them. One, without a doubt, was Alwin Schockemöhle – Alwin could do things with horses that nobody else could do.

'Draw-reins are an aid to help you supple the horse and get him in the right shape, and handled properly, I think they do absolutely no harm. If a horse is built the right way naturally you're not going to hurt him, because even though you might move his head this way and that, it will always come back to the natural position. No horse that I know of has ever had his head stuck on the floor.

'Where the danger lies is if you just hang on the mouth to pull the head down, because you are working on the one area you want to keep as soft as you can, the mouth. There is a certain amount of credibility for the standing martingale in this respect, because the draw-reins should not be used to hold the head down; rather, they should be used to work the head down in a soft manner.

'Having got the head down, the second part of the operation – and this is absolutely tantamount to its overall success – is that the back end of the horse has to be moved up. It's no good having the head down and the back end in the next parish. You must be able to work the horse so that his hocks are right up underneath him: if you've got the head down and the hocks under him, you are winding up the screw, the explosive element of the horse as far as jumping is concerned.'

How does David achieve all this?

'You hold the draw-reins outside the little finger and the snaffle rein, ideally between the first and second fingers. Then if the horse is getting solid and you want his head down a bit lower, you let the snaffle rein slip. You will finish up with an armful of rein quite quickly, and then you have to shorten everything up again.

'I believe you should be able to put a horse's head anywhere you want it at any time. If you're not in control of the head, you're not in control of the horse. So the option should be mine, to put his head wherever I want it – just a little bit of extra pressure and he'll give to it. If he wants to put his head down, I reward him with extra rein, then he stays soft.

'So, you've got him totally relaxed and he's cantering around with his head on the floor, but his back end is in the next parish. That's all very nice for a little reward, but then you tell him "Now then, lad, business starts". You gather him up again and use your circles and squares, shoulder-in and half-pass to get his hocks underneath him. When you've got his head down, sit into him on a circle and you will feel him coming up underneath you – he can't go round a small circle if he's got his head down but is *long* – he'll fall over. So you squeeze him up with your legs and get him a bit more active – there's no particular secret to it.

'When you bring his hocks up underneath him like that, it's like coiling up a spring. When he's working properly you can put his

🐎 'The draw-reins are fitted so that the rein passes inside the "V" of the running martingale to prevent the horse's front foot catching in it when jumping (inset). Here the horse has set himself against the reins and is heavy in the hand, and his hocks are not coming underneath him. This is typical of the problems caused by Lannegan's particular conformation, and I continually have to work to counteract it.'

head where you like, with your bottom finger on the draw-rein, and he's soft and supple, with his hocks underneath him. Then you've got the ultimate, with him cantering along like a lovely, bouncing ball. You've got something to operate with, because the spring is coiled up as much as you can get it and he's ready for action and under control.'

The 'wise man on the ground'

David's own skill in training with draw-reins is well known, but when he is working in the school, whether at flatwork or jumping, he will often call on either Marysia or Emma to watch, and will ask for their observations on how the horse is going. He points out the importance of having knowledgeable advice from the floor. 'If you are working with draw-reins, you need somebody with a bit of knowledge watching you. Often people will put a draw-rein on and the horse will get his head set in one spot and never move it. That's useless. Or when someone pulls the head down and the back end is way behind them, that's useless, too.

'It's the same with anything you are trying

to do with any part of the horse, if the work is useless, it's useless. To develop it properly, you have to adjust *mentally* to the situation you find yourself in. You have a picture in your mind, then you make adjustments to get what you want, with whatever tack you put on, to make the horse do what you want him to do. Don't forget that you are dominating him so that he performs in a technique which *you* want him to follow, within reason.

'That is why when you go to a show and watch a horse going round the ring from a distance, if it's a well known rider you can tell who it is by looking at the way the horse is going. We all have our own little computer which controls how we adjust to a fence we are going to jump. By watching the horse, you can tell whose computer is controlling it – that's the way I always put it.'

A mistake that many people make, David points out, is to use a particular piece of tack because they think it will solve a problem, but without any real appreciation of what is actually happening to the horse, or how it is adapting to it. 'That is why a wise man on the ground is so important to you – someone who can say do this or that, or the horse is not doing this or that.' It is also clear from watching David work that, with the possible exception of draw-reins, no 'gadgets' or artificial aids are used continuously; once they have served their purpose of correcting a problem they are removed, and only re-introduced temporarily when necessary.

Cooling down

Normally, schooling lessons shouldn't need to be too long, David feels. 'You don't want to over-dominate all the time. Keep it pleasant; keep the horse enjoying it, if you can. If he's naughty then we go to the necessary lengths to correct him, but everything wants to be fun, within reason, just always bringing in that little bit more discipline. If I have a fault, it is probably that I don't do quite enough; but particularly with a young horse, you don't want to overdo it.

'If you're working and the horse does a piece of good work, pat him and leave it be. It's a good thing to know when enough is enough, both when the horse is going well *and* when he's going badly, because the situation can so easily deteriorate further. You might sort out the problem eventually, but the horse is not going to get any better at that point. Put him away that day.'

At the end of a schooling session David insists that the horses are properly cooled down, by taking them out of the school and walking them. 'Harvey [Smith] will have them walk round for an hour, to get everything settled down. This is where a walking machine could be quite useful, to walk the horses for half-an-hour instead of the girls having to ride them.

It's just to let the metabolism get back to normal.'

Cooling down is just as important after a competition. 'I've seen Alwin go in three from last in a jump-off. He'll jump a fantastic round against the clock and go into the lead, then come out and where most of us would jump off our horses to see if the last two riders were going to beat us, Alwin will go back to the collecting ring and do five minutes work to steady his horse down. To me, that is the ultimate professional at work.

'There is a lot of mental as well as physical pressure on the horse. If you're going against the clock and you've got a quick or sensitive horse, it could really wind him up to turn him round and kick him on, and turn him and find you've got a long one, which upsets the rhythm because you give him a kick which he doesn't usually get – then he might want to be off. Then you want to turn back, so you screw him round again – so you've over-pressurised him in every direction and he can't handle it.

'This is what you *mustn't* do with novices, and why so many novices are ruined when they go against the clock. They're abused before they are ready for it, and mentally they can't adjust.'

4
JUMP SCHOOLING

Although classic principles underlie all the work David does with his horses, the novices coming into the yard do not follow any set pattern of jump schooling. As always, the emphasis is on treating each horse as an individual and doing what seems necessary, or beneficial to its progress day by day. Since a horse will have to have demonstrated a fairly high degree of proficiency and natural jumping talent to have been accepted into the yard in the first place, there will be little, if any, work with trotting poles or cavaletti. The aim is to school the horse on the flat to build up its strength, power and athleticism to cope with jumping fences with a rider, and it is its ability to do that which David puts to the test.

He does of course appreciate the value of other types of exercises, and will use them if he thinks they might help a particular situation. 'You do what you think is right to achieve your goal. There must be many ways of doing this, and what we do just happens to be our way. After seeing the Cadre Noir I went through a stage of putting driving reins on two or three horses, and we then lunged them over a fence with a placing pole. It was useful with one particular horse, but we've never done it since.

'It's the same with loose schooling – we'll do it occasionally, if the notion takes us. We did it with some three-year-olds once, and what we found was that different ones went better on different days, depending on what happened, or how each one felt on a particular day.'

Schooling at home

David's aim is to improve each horse's style and technique over fences at home so that in the show-ring the horse will meet the minimum of surprises and be able to adapt himself to negotiate the different types of obstacle successfully. There is constant emphasis on keeping everything simple and making training enjoyable for the horse. This does not mean the work is too easy – horses have to concentrate and do their best – but they will never be faced with anything that is too difficult for their scope or level of ability, nor be asked too many different questions in the same training session.

The indoor school, where most of the work is done, contains the minimum of practice fences – enough stands to set up a grid, and enough poles to create a variety of exercises. However, in order to teach a horse about the show-ring environment when he will tackle a complete course and jump in a strange situation away from home, David will often arrange to use the facilities of local indoor shows, schooling horses over the fences set up for the competitions on the day following the show. He feels there is no point in jumping horses excessively over home-made courses, since they will become too accustomed to what they are doing at home and may well react completely differently when taken to a show. How often do riders complain 'My horse jumps perfectly at home, but won't look at a fence when he gets to a show!'?

Jump schooling at home is therefore designed to build up confidence and to overcome specific problems encountered by individual horses. This applies as much to the older horses as to the younger ones, since schooling and training is a dynamic process, needing continual reappraisal and reinforcement.

Technique and gridwork

In the earliest stages the emphasis is on 'making a nice shape' over a fence, and the simplest of obstacles will be used. 'We'll put up a cross or two, with a pole on the floor and a pole behind, then gradually build up to verticals, and see how it goes.'

The first fence is always a cross: it helps to keep the horse straight and encourages him to jump the fence at the centre. A placing pole 6ft from the fence will 'set him up a bit' and ensure that he approaches the fence on the right stride. 'Even when you are loose jumping you should put up a tiny cross-pole one or two strides from a fence, so when the horse gets to the fence, you know he's always right,' David explains.

'Mistakes *will* happen, so you've got to adjust things to get the stride correct. A horse's stride is ten to twelve foot long, so there is an area where you can either stand back and take off, or get in that bit deeper.

Within that space, something has to happen – and that is what the training is all about: to get "that bit" about right. In the hunter classes in America the idea is that you can do eight strides in seven, or seven strides in eight, and the stride should look perfectly even. Ideally that is how it should be, very kind to the eye and very easy to the horse.'

To have the horse concentrating and jumping straight, cross-poles can be adapted from a low to a high cross; this will give a horse the ideal lead into a progressively built grid. Not only does gridwork help to improve a horse's suppleness and concentration, it is also a valuable technique for assessing and regulating stride length, for the rider as much as for the horse, and David often uses it to improve the technique of participants at the lecture/demonstrations he is frequently asked to give during the winter.

A typical method of building up a grid

jump schooling

would be to start with a placing pole 6ft in front of a small cross, followed by a 10ft space for a bounce to a second cross. For his own show jumpers David knows exactly what would be a sensible starting height for them to jump in a schooling session. For unknown horses, however, he will always start at a low height, even if they are experienced jumpers; and he will increase the height of the fences progressively, working on the principle that 'it is embarrassing if you start too high and have to put the fences down!'

There will be a stride to a small vertical, then one stride to a parallel, and another stride to another parallel to complete the grid. However, no new fence is added until the horse is taking the previous jumps confidently and accurately. Building up a grid to improve a horse's way of going is an art, and the number and design of the fences and the distances between them have to be tailored to invite the horse to improve his performance. A smaller, cobby horse for example will cover less ground in a stride than a big 16.3hh Warmblood, and although both might tackle the same course in the jumping arena, a grid for training purposes would need to be built differently for each horse.

'It's up to the rider to take the horse to the fence and put him in the right place,' says David. 'And it's the pole that he's jumping that gets him off the ground. All you are try-ing to do is to make the horse think for himself. When you are training, aim at making the horse go a bit closer to the fence. Remember that you *are* training, so you don't want him going too fast or standing off. When we do gridwork, we always concentrate on tight strides rather than long ones.'

Varying the composition of the fences and the number of strides between them, and using placing poles, all make this method of improving jumping style and correcting problems more versatile. Thus the fence of cross-poles helps the horse approach the middle of the fence and sets him up to continue down the line. 'A bounce in front of a fence makes a horse concentrate,' adds David. 'And if he is jumping with his head in the air, put a plank (in preference to a pole, as it is safer should the horse land on it) ten foot out from the fence – it will make the horse look in order to jump inside it.'

In jumping, as in flatwork, the horse needs to be settled and to concentrate on his work to be successful. David achieves this by working calmly on one problem at a time and being careful not to ask too much at once, so the horse never becomes confused or flustered. This point cannot be emphasised too strongly, since riders often have difficulty in identifying a particular problem and then working to overcome it. If the rider does not understand why a horse is in trouble, he cannot know how to help him.

Schooling on a figure-eight

One of David's favourite jumping exercises for novice horses is to put up a single fence in the centre of a figure-of-eight track, which can be jumped several times in succession from both directions. This can be used to teach the horse to approach from either direction, at an angle, and to land on the correct leading leg ready for the turn away from the fence on the opposite rein. The exercise can be made easy or difficult, depending upon the height and design of the fence. The concentration needed to continue in the figure-of-eight helps to keep the horse settled and under con-trol; it also quickly shows up any problems, since good rhythm and balance are needed to place the horse accurately and with sufficient impulsion at each approach.

The young horse Showman, brought over from Ireland and showing considerable promise, needed to have his technique sharpened up. A big, handsome horse with tremendous potential scope, he was inclined to be lazy, particularly over smaller fences, so his jump schooling at home concentrated on improving this situation; and the figure-eight exercise proved to be a valuable exercise for him.

Working on a figure-of-eight: 'Showman approaching a small cross parallel on the left rein, jumping the oxer and landing to go into a right turn. He will complete the right-handed circle and return to jump again on the right rein. The steep cross makes him think about the jump and be more careful and athletic.'

Beginning with a single cross-pole, David first approached the fence almost straight. Once Showman grasped the idea of circling back to the fence and jumping it from both directions, the fence was widened to a double cross, demanding more effort but still encouraging the horse to jump it centrally. Gradually David increased the angle of approach and the height of the cross so that it gave Showman something to think about; he had to concentrate really hard on the question he was being asked, with the result that he lifted his front legs more tidily and put in a stronger effort over the fence, really using himself athletically, instead of treating the fence with disdain.

Schooling over a combination

Another exercise for Showman was set up to persuade him to back off his fences more, and again, to tackle them with greater care and effort: two fences were placed with three strides between them (16 yards apart). At first, going fairly slowly, Showman put in four strides. Then the fences were raised and tackled with more speed – though still of course, maintaining balance and rhythm. The increased intensity of the exercise forced Showman to concentrate more, take off correctly at the first fence, cover the distance to the second in the required three strides, and use a more rounded, athletic outline to negotiate it. The combination was jumped no more than half-a-dozen times, and David stopped as soon as Showman coped with the exercise well; there's no point in over-doing an exercise once the horse has mastered it. The lesson lasted no more than half-an-hour, underlining David's belief that 'if they do it well once or twice, that's enough'.

Planning the youngster's early career

At home, David firmly believes that once or twice a week is enough to jump school young horses; he also warns that at a show a novice can be badly frightened by being asked to jump fences that are too big too soon. But equally . . . 'if a horse has the potential to go on to another level, you can also stay at the lower level for too long. If you jump a horse long enough over three feet high, in the end he'll think he can't jump any higher than that. To me it is one of the most exciting things of all, when you produce a young horse and you're moving from one Grade up to the next and he handles it. There's a terrific kick to that.'

An example of this was when Showman began to fulfil his promise jumping abroad later in the year. 'When I jumped Showman at Bremen, he jumped the 1.50m course. In the first place, he shouldn't have been in it, but when he jumped a clear round, then another clear round in the jump-off, I wouldn't have been happier if I'd won the Grand Prix. He did it with good heart and good style. That to me gives more satisfaction now than anything – you know you are doing your job properly if you are getting that kind of performance out of them.'

The novice horses' first competitions these days are likely to be at Newcomer and Foxhunter level, though David is not completely happy with the type of competitions available. 'I think the courses are actually too small these days. In the past you used to start off at Grade C with your novices. The courses weren't complicated – you would have three up, three down and one in the middle, or something like that. That is how you started your horses off and if a fence had a bit of size to it, as long as you had plenty of room to get at it, that was all right.

'These days they try to give you distance problems, often into a combination, and this is far too complicated for novices. A novice class needs to be straightforward – obviously a bit higher than they tend to be – with different fences, a good gate or a good set of poles.'

Understanding distance-related fences

Understanding the distances between fences and how to ride them has obviously become increasingly important. 'The normal stride in the show-ring for a big horse is twelve feet', David explains. 'I always measure distances from the first stand to the next stand. When the distance is more than two strides, I measure from where the horse lands to where I want him to take off, or where he will take off. That is always in multiples of four of my strides, because four of my strides make one of the horse's strides, which is roughly twelve feet. That would be for anything other than combinations.

'I've got my own way of measuring combinations, which I've never altered and it works perfectly for me. I try to walk to what I consider the highest point of the horse's jump, so if it is a vertical, that is directly above it. If it is a parallel going in, I take my distance from not quite the back pole, but just over halfway through the parallel. I walk then to the back pole of whatever we have to jump out, working on the theory that it is always the back

pole that turns you over.

'Harvey and I both use the same system and it works for us. If it is a very wide parallel going out on a short distance, obviously we are aware that we have to be very together going in; but the system never lies to us and I think our conversion to a triple bar is better, because if you only walk the inside distance you are missing out the bit where the horse is actually going over.

'I don't think it makes any difference where you actually measure from, however, as long as you know how to interpret the measurements and how they affect your horse.'

One method David uses to teach riders to see a stride is to put up two fences with a four-stride distance and have them ride it in both four and five strides, to appreciate the difference. However: 'The best advice I could give anyone about distances, especially when they get longer, on six or eight strides, is yes, do the theory, but at the end of the day, use your eye. It is your eye that will save your neck, not the theory!'

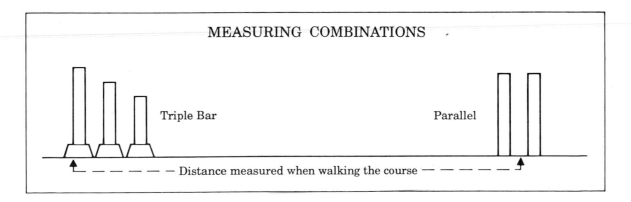

MEASURING COMBINATIONS

Triple Bar

Parallel

← – – – – – Distance measured when walking the course – – – – – →

'This sequence shows how a placing pole can be used to encourage the horse to land on the correct leg for the turn to the next fence.'

Rider technique

'Seeing a stride' is an ability which eludes many jumping riders, causing immense frustration; nor is it something which is easy to teach, and it isn't the same for every rider. David tries to explain: 'I believe there is a little computer in every rider's brain which is programmed to jump fences. If you watch John Whitaker ride, or Michael, Nick, Harvey or myself – if you watch the *horse* go, you can tell which of us is riding it. That means we all ride to a fence a little bit differently, because we each have our own programmed method that we dictate to the horse on the approach to a fence. There are a lot of similarities, but you still recognise the styles as being different one from another, even jumping at such a high level.

'The American system is different again, based on their hunter classes and equitation – if it's an eight-stride distance, it's got to be ridden in eight perfect strides. The Americans can actually walk distances round corners, whereas I don't think any of our boys would have a clue about walking a distance round a corner and I certainly wouldn't know how to do it – yet there is nobody better at jumping against the clock than John, Michael or Nick.'

In the final analysis, David comes back to the essential ingredient of 'feel'. 'The feel for the thing is that you're balanced right, so that it fits the pattern to go forward or ease up, or to know that you're completely wrong and check strongly. I think a lot of people *know* when they haven't got a good stride, but don't know what to do about it. That is why I like to do the exercise of jumping two fences in four and five strides – if I'm teaching somebody, it helps me to know how good they are at seeing things.'

The importance of getting this right is demonstrated by an example of a student jumping at an indoor show. 'He did two strides in a three-stride distance and he had the next fence down – because he had gone forward on two to jump a three, the horse had become too opened up and he paid the penalty.

'That is why, in a jump-off against the clock, you don't normally take a stride out to the second fence because it dictates to you the rest of the round. Once you get the old computer opened up to big strides, normally you keep going on bigger ones. Otherwise it upsets the horse's rhythm.

'If you take a stride out to the last fence it doesn't matter. All you've got to do is land and canter or gallop through the finish and you've

got all day to get the horse shortened up again. But if you do it earlier, you'll pay the penalty nine times out of ten – unless you've got a horse like a Milton, who can make four out of five and not know he's done it! These special horses can take a stride out and not even know.'

Although actually 'seeing a stride' in the heat of competition is a talent not everyone finds they possess, much of the horse's schooling is designed to help the situation, by teaching him to shorten his stride when necessary. 'A shorter-striding horse is not going to be so far out coming to a fence as a longer-striding one, as if he is that far out, he will put another stride in,' David points out.

His son Matthew is a keen young show jumper and much of his pony's schooling concerns shortening his stride. 'We make him do little circles, get his pony shortened up and canter down the line, then circle again half-way down, just generally working on getting his stride a lot shorter.'

Ponies – which soon become very knowing – have their own special problems. 'For

'As seen in this photograph the stress on the foreleg joints on landing is enormous.'

'My nearly open hand shows how little pressure needs to be on the draw-rein when jumping.'

children up to a certain age it's a matter of steering and surviving. We make them go round things at the end of the school so they don't cut corners. That's very important, because ponies will set off towards the far end and very often be on their way back long before they've reached it!'

Different types of fence present different problems, but the basic approach, David says, does not vary much. 'A horse has to work a bit harder at an oxer, and a triple bar is a lot easier than a parallel – that is why a front rail must never be higher than a back rail – it's the most difficult thing to get a horse to jump higher in front than behind.

'You have to be softer to a vertical. It's lovely to ride a big vertical, or to see a horse jump a big vertical. There's a great art in it, the approach has to be absolutely perfect. I think there is much more art in jumping a big vertical than a big parallel.'

Making the right approach is the essence of the successful show-jumping rider's job. 'The rider has to dictate the pace and the rhythm to the horse. You should work everything from a rhythm. Then if you get the stride right for the horse as you present him at the fence, all that helps dictate to the horse his technique as he jumps it. He's got to lengthen and shorten, coming to it, and in those ways, you help him. You can take it a bit further and so-called "lift him off the floor", but a horse basically has to jump the fence himself.

If he's a decent horse, he'll jump it for you, as long as you've done your job correctly in getting him there.'

Once the horse is in the air, landing and turning in the right direction is the next part of the equation. The design of jump-off courses nowadays has placed increasingly heavy demands on the horse's ability to turn at speed, and the idea of turning while the horse is in the air has gained ground.

'I find this very difficult, because I was always taught that you land before you turn,' is David's firm view. 'You land squarely, take a stride and then turn. But course builders these days, especially indoors, dictate a lot of turns inside fences when you land. If you're going against the clock, you start turning in the air, so you land on one leg and you're turning on it. It's wonderful stuff, until you break the horse down.

'A horse should always land on the correct leg for the turn he's going to make. There are various things you can do, if he always lands on a particular leg, to make him get used to the idea that perhaps he should land on one leg rather than the other. For instance you can jump him on an angle, using the wall of the school as a guide to tell him he's got to go one way. Or you can have a fence, say an oxer, and you want to turn after it, so you put a pole on the floor at an angle after the fence, so that as he lands he sees the pole and veers away from it.'

 # Dealing with problems

Even when the training has been done well and the rider is talented, with horses there is no guarantee of success. A number of things can go wrong, for some of which the rider is to blame, while others can be the horse's problem, not necessarily because the horse misbehaves, but perhaps he doesn't always understand what is needed, or perhaps he simply doesn't have the skill and scope to perform as asked. Just as a human being can be unsuccessful with the wrong career choice, so can a horse. Other problems may simply be

a question of further training and improving the horse's technique. So what can be done about them?

'If a horse jumps flat, put him in deeper to the fence, to get him to round up his back. The worst thing you can do is to stand back.

'If a horse dangles a leg, or worse still, leaves a leg down, I've always found that that is a confidence problem. A horse that persisted in leaving a leg down every time would be useless, you would never jump it, but obviously if it only does it once in a while, you can discourage the habit. Never build a practice fence that will encourage him to leave a leg down, such as a straight vertical. If you get a bit too close, his immediate reaction is to leave a leg down to protect himself. But of course it doesn't protect him – it aggravates the situation and he hits it for six.

'So always build schooling fences with a 'V' in front, then you never give him the excuse to leave a leg down. But in competition you must always be careful with a horse like that, because if he ever panics, he will do it again.'

David recalls an incident at the Barcelona Olympics concerning an enormous combination which only three horses tackled successfully and which attracted considerable criticism.

'Some horses will "paddle" an oxer. At the Olympic Games at Barcelona, on the last day, there was a big combination. When Michael Whitaker was jumping Mon Santa, the horse only made the first pole of the third part – he never intended to jump the back pole, but he didn't paddle, he just chested it out and was very safe. But a couple of the horses started to paddle and they're terribly dangerous when that happens because if they get a pole between their legs they can go head over heels.'

If a horse stands off a fence too much, says David: 'That's your fault. You mustn't let him. You control the approach and dictate the technique.

'Hesitating or stopping can be due to a number of things. The horse might be chicken-hearted, he might be stubborn, he might be scared. It's up to you to interpret it and come up with the answers as to why he's stopping. He might just be nappy. Some will nap on corners, or they won't go forward, or they'll run out. Sometimes they've been overfaced and don't want to jump. Sorting it out is all part of your relationship with the horse.'

In dealing with problems, as with every other aspect of the show-jumper's training, David's views constantly emphasise the necessity to treat horses as living, breathing individuals, and not as machines for winning prizes. Only with this concerned and perceptive approach will the aspiring show-jumping rider have any chance of success. Young horses are often produced through the winter indoor jumping season, but David also warns against too much indoor jumping.

'A lot of people produce young horses indoors. They start off at the beginning of the winter and by the end of it they've won a thousand pounds indoors. I don't think that is terribly beneficial to the horse. It's good to introduce him to the sport indoors, but if you drill him indoors, then take him outside, he is a completely different animal, so I think most of his jumping should be done outside. For experience, jumping outside is worth three times what he learns jumping inside – a lot of problems are camouflaged jumping indoors.'

Jumping against time

As well as training to improve the horse's technique, getting the approach right and correctly measuring strides and distances, a further aspect of successful show jumping is timing, not only against the clock, but in riding the competition accurately within the allowed time. 'The first rider in doesn't really know from the time allowed, how the course will ride. You can have a look at the time allowed, then walk the course and think, for instance, "68 seconds – that's a bit tight", but you don't really know. So everybody else asks

the first couple of riders to go "What's the time like?" – it depends on how the course builder has measured it. Grand Prix and Nations Cups are 400 metres per minute, which is quite quick. A lot of courses have been ruined because the time hasn't been worked out quite right. Two or three seconds on a course of 80 seconds can make a tremendous difference.

'With normal indoor shows, the time is usually quite all right. On outdoor courses, the course builder can be naughty, depending

jump schooling

on the type of course. If there are a couple of places where the walker with the wheel has gone round a fence and in fact you can turn on the inside, you can save time. But if there are a lot of straight lines to verticals, that's when you are adding strides and then the clock goes ever so quickly and *that* is when you can get into trouble – so you do have to be aware of that.'

David believes that in today's show-jumping world, novice horses are often asked to go against the clock too frequently and too soon; particular care therefore needs to be taken not to ask too much of a potentially good horse before he is ready, and so upset him. Part of David's own skill lies in his ability to nurse a horse around a course at speed, without appearing to go particularly fast and whilst making the jumping look effortless. 'I think if you get the rhythm and take the shortest route, you're trying to ride the course in the nicest possible way, the easiest for your horse. That's where all this training comes in, to get it like that.'

5
TEACHING THE SHOWJUMPING RIDER

There is a saying 'Those who can, do; those who can't, teach' and in the horse world, it often happens that the excellent trainers are people who have never quite made it to the top competitively, but in their strenuous efforts to do so, have acquired a vast amount of knowledge and understanding and are able to help others with their problems.

David Broome – the man whose 'natural' talent took him to the top at an early age and then kept him there – has a rather different approach, and may be the exception that proves the general rule. In the early 1990s he is increasingly in demand as a teacher, passing on his philosophy – for it is a philosophy rather than a set technique – to the young and ambitious riders who seek his help. 'He is different from anybody else,' said one young rider from India who had come West to try to make it in the tough, competitive world of show jumping – thus summing up succinctly, if unwittingly, the whole of the myth and methodology that comprises the David Broome enigma.

Broome: teacher unique

Some aspects of 'life as applied to show jumping' are never allowed to be forgotten around David's yard and the importance of keeping a sense of proportion and a sense of humour is one of them. Another foreign student left a message for David on his departure after three months' stay: 'Tell him he's the best teacher I've ever had.'

'I'm the *only* teacher he's ever had!' quipped David in response.

The international show season now extends from April to Christmas, and once the Grade A horses are back in work, there is little time for anything but schooling and competing. The first three months of the year, however, are quieter and this is the period when David is available for teaching, not only at home, but also giving lecture/demonstrations all over the country. The usual format for these is for David to assess and advise several 'guinea pig' riders with their own horses, and usually in front of a packed audience. Then he will give a demonstration on one of his own horses, and answer questions. These are the occasions when all sorts of golden gems of advice can be picked up and remembered later by the truly keen rider. Here are some examples:

'If you buy a horse you are not keen on when you first see it, you will be unforgiving when it makes a mistake later on. You have got to love it.'

'I'm always wary of people without martingales ...'

'If I'm working a horse outside, I often canter a circle on an incline – half going up and half going down. It makes the horse work a lot harder, makes him use himself.'

'If you watch the top riders at a show, their horses are always light and free. Everything they do is for a reason. Watching them is a very cheap lesson.'

'All you're trying to do is make the horse think for himself.'

'It's important to know where the horse's legs are.'

'We work the horses on the flat much more than over fences. Everything starts on the floor.'

'Jumps in the collecting ring are only for the rider. If the horse is nice and supple and loose, a couple of pops are enough. It's stupid to leave your best jumps in the collecting ring.'

'To get a stride right, you have to sit right – heels down and toes in.'

'Heels down and toes in' is in the best tradition of British riding of course, and to David, it is the basis of his assessment when he first looks at any horse and rider. 'Whether it's a cowboy in a film or anybody else, if I look at someone on a horse I start at the feet – then you know if they can ride or not. The heel has got to be down a bit.'

Whilst recognising that methods vary the world over, David deplores the American style of riding with the toe turned slightly out, enabling the rider to grip with the calf. 'If you grip with your calf, everything gets tensed up. I think it looks awful, and it's dangerous – just see what happens when you go through a doorway and your toe is out,' he states bluntly. 'I think it all starts with the feet.'

'Heels down' is also a refrain known to every young Pony Club rider and the Pony Club is where Emma Lipscomb – eighteen and one of David's grooms – had her early grounding in horsemanship. A good all-round rider, she took part in Pony Club mounted games, show jumping and cross-country riding. Now she is learning to ride David's horses and others in the yard the way he likes them ridden, so that she can help head girl Emma Storey with exercising and schooling. In the rest of this chapter we shall describe David's teaching methods and advice to riders using Emma's tuition as an example. The horse Emma rides in the lesson is a young mare inclined to be quick and sharp, one which needs encouragement to relax and settle to her work.

The first thing David points out is the importance of paying attention to the horse at

teaching the showjumping rider

'I think this is quite a good position. My heels are down, toes in, a lot of my body weight is "down my legs" and I can probably just see about an inch of my toe in front of my knee. I hope this is a seat my father would be proud of!'

all times and taking no chances, regardless of how quiet the horse is or how well the rider knows it. 'More accidents are caused on quiet horses than on wild ones. On a quiet horse you take advantage, but you never have a bad accident on a bad one because you are paying one hundred per cent attention to what you are doing.'

A key to David's security in the saddle and therefore the effectiveness of his seat, is what he explains as 'having my body weight "down my legs"'. To achieve this the rider's joints must be kept flexible – it is tension which causes the inexperienced competitor to stiffen up and bounce in the saddle and so become unbalanced.

Basic rider position

Emma begins by walking the mare round the school, while David considers her position. 'She has all her weight on her bottom, with no weight down her legs and she's riding a little bit short. I wouldn't have thought she has a lot of strength in her legs,' he observes, then asks Emma 'Is that fair comment?'

The stirrups are adjusted and David advises 'Get more weight down your legs and get them in a better position with your knees in – don't grip with the inside of your calf.

'When you are sitting up straight, you should be able to see about an inch of your toe. If a rider has no weight in his feet, all his weight is on his bottom and he's just going to bounce around. But if he lets the weight drop down through his legs, then it is evenly distributed either side of the horse. He's going to be a lot more secure and a lot more comfortable, too.

'If you look at John Wayne in the saddle – he may be sitting there twelve hours in a day – he's relaxed and part of his horse.'

As Emma sets off again, he comments 'We'll give her five for the smile! She ought to keep her eyes on the horse's ears, to know what is happening, but the horse is quite happy.'

This last observation emphasises how greatly riding ability varies, and how easy it is to blame a horse for misbehaviour which is really the fault of an unskilled, unobservant

'Emma sits a little bit round-shouldered, and her legs are a little far back. She needs to lift her shoulders and get her weight down through her legs to make the work easier for both horse and rider and give a more pleasing picture.'

rider. Most horses are willing to work correctly and calmly when given clear and precise instructions, or 'aids', by the rider, and by watching different riders on one horse, David can quickly pinpoint not only a rider's general ability, but any potential problems.

The other obvious conclusion from this situation is that whereas most riders tend to believe their problems lie with the horse, it is usually the rider who needs reschooling! Many horses could be saved from psychological and physical trauma, or being repeatedly sold on, or ruined completely, if their riders would devote a little of the time and money they spend on gadgets, or even new horses, on obtaining some professional advice on their own riding. It is never too late to learn, and even the top riders continually advise each other and discuss their various problems among themselves.

David, who has been riding since the age of two, has developed what is referred to as a 'natural' seat. In fact it is simply the most effective position from which to control the horse, and because he is able to maintain it whilst working his horse at all paces, it makes him look part of the horse (hence the word 'natural'). Young riders could learn much from studying David's riding position. His seat is firmly settled, yet relaxed, in the deepest part of the saddle, and his body is upright with his spine vertical; he keeps his head up so that he doesn't become unbalanced. He does not slouch, but carries his body erect, with his shoulders square and his upper arms relaxed at his sides, elbows in and bent, with the hands carried to handle the reins with lightness. His legs tend to be forward in traditional British style, but carry the weight of his body down either side of his horse to the stirrup, not pressing heavily on the stirrup, but letting his heel fall naturally downwards, with his toe pointing straight ahead. His overall appearance is one of relaxed readiness for action, poised to be flexible, but not tense. Tension means that it is impossible to make smooth, subtle movements to give precise aids.

Teacher relationship

Emma has already achieved some improvement. 'She's done what we've told her to do,' David approves – and of course, the ability of the rider to understand and put into practice what the teacher advises is another important aspect of learning. 'She's sitting better in the saddle, with more weight down her legs – she'd look quite good now, in the Pony Club!'

The gentle quip is all part of David's way of putting a student at ease – it can be quite nerve-wracking to have a renowned world expert watching you ride, and the student needs to be relaxed and comfortable to have any chance of riding competently. David knows that to make a student smile has the effect of making him relax in the saddle, when he will be able to use his body effectively, whereas a tense rider not only loses control over his own seat, hands and legs, but also communicates his tenseness to the horse.

Once satisfied with Emma's basic position at the walk, David sends her forward into trot. She sits upright and quiet in the saddle and the mare moves steadily with a nice cadence. However, her head is rather high and fixed in position. David tells Emma to work her wrists quietly, moving the bit gently backwards and forwards across the horse's tongue. 'It's more a wrist movement than an arm movement.'

The mare has been tacked up in the basic schooling equipment of snaffle bridle, flash noseband, running martingale and draw-reins; she also wears tendon boots. David has checked the fit of the saddle, and also delivered a ticking off about a horse which was tacked up in a badly fitting saddle the previous day.

He explains how he was taught to hold the reins, and why. 'The thumbs are on top, the bottom rein around the outside of the little finger, and the top rein between the second and third, or third and fourth finger – then when you want the bottom rein to come in contact, you just tilt your hand.' The 'bottom' rein referred to is the draw-rein, and the 'top' rein the snaffle rein. 'If I want to shorten the horse on the draw-rein, I let the top rein slide through my fingers. Then, when all of a sudden something happens, you have to shorten up everything quickly.'

David asks Emma to change the rein, which she does, remembering to change her diagonal and David watches her quietly for a few moments. He is a great believer in letting the rider ride the horse, unlike many teachers who almost try to do the riding themselves from the ground. He is also careful not to deluge the rider with too many different instructions in succession, which frequently ends up with the rider trying too hard and becoming tense and confused as he tries to remember too many things at once, and force his body to make the changes. David's approach to teaching the rider is exactly the same as when training a horse, so that as far as possible, without the horse becoming unmanageable, he takes one thing at a time.

 # Working in

With both the horse and Emma settled, it is time to start work, beginning with circles at the trot. 'Remember, you're keeping that rein light,' David reminds her. The mare begins to run a little and David instructs, 'Don't let her rush off with you, turn her head to the outside a little bit'. This doesn't have any significant effect and David immediately changes tactics. 'Tell you what – do a square. Steady her up if she's getting on her forehand. Steady, steady,' he encourages the mare.

'A square is more useful in a way, because you go in a straight line, then turn, then a straight line, then turn and the horse doesn't get its head set on the circle,' David explains. However, for the moment the mare is not responding. Being young and sensitive, it takes very little to upset and excite her. 'She's not doing that very well, Emma', David observes. 'You haven't got much of a square. Go to the wall, then a right angle, then straight.'

Emma makes a determined effort, and the mare overcorrects and almost turns the opposite way at the wall. Everyone laughs. 'We'll forgive you that one,' David calls, then sets about putting matters right. 'Is she getting a bit boiled up?' he asks.

'Yes,' answers Emma.

'Try the other way then, and steady her. Try to get her to relax so you can let the reins go a little bit more.' He explains further. 'You need to get her head a bit lower with the draw-reins. Because she wants to be sharp, you want to try to make her sloppy, so work the draw-reins a little more. Every time you want to turn, take up the draw-rein, then when she straightens up after the turn, give her the rein. You can let the top rein slip through your fingers.'

There is an improvement, but Emma isn't happy. 'Then she escapes,' she tells David.

'Turn her then, she's got to come round and she can't go on her forehand. But you've let the reins go a little bit dead – keep working them quietly, and as you go round on the circle, turn her head a little bit one way, then the other. Then the mare will give to you, then you give to her a little bit, and hopefully she will keep her head down. You've got to keep on doing it – take and then give, and you'll get her head a bit lower again.

'Be careful with your legs. She'll go more kindly to your voice than to your legs – your legs can nearly stay still with this mare. Talk to her, calm her down and encourage her.'

After a few minutes the mare settles much better; she has realised that this rider is not going to hurt her, and she understands what she is being asked. All that is required is for her to go quietly, paying attention and with the beginnings of the outline considered 'correct' for a show jumper on the flat, which David describes as 'a bridge, from nose to tail'.

Suppling exercises

Show-jumping horses are often criticised for being 'overbent' and it is true to say that when they are being worked on the flat, they are more likely to be overbent than above the bit. However, it should be remembered that one of the main requirements of the show-jumping horse is great suppleness, with the ability to jump, gallop, pull up and turn its large, heavy body very fast in a very small space; and although in a perfect world all horses would always go absolutely correctly, the over-exaggeration of some of the things the rider is trying to achieve is an inevitable feature of training in a less-than-perfect world. Some exercises, such as turning the head to one side and then the other whilst riding on a circle, to prevent the horse's head from becoming 'fixed' and inflexible in position, are well outside the sphere of classical equestrianism; but given the type of show-jumping courses built today, they have their place in the specialised training of the show-jumping horse.

When Emma has completed several circles calmly on each rein, with the mare lowering her head and relaxing, David gives her a lateral exercise, just asking the mare to move away from the leg as she travels down the school, the beginning of a half-pass movement. This is quite difficult to do, and Emma immediately falls into the error of tensing the leg she is trying to use so that the weight comes off the stirrup.

'Your legs are wobbling a little bit,' David points out. 'The stirrup is loose on your foot. You can bring your leg back and still keep the weight on it – push a bit more weight down on to your stirrups.' While Emma perseveres with the new instruction, David explains: 'It's natural to slouch a bit on the saddle and let it take your weight, but it isn't any good. If you've got the weight down your legs you become part of the horse, instead of on top of him. You start to fit into the horse and there is no effort in it, so you don't wear yourself out doing it.'

Slouching in the saddle in the effort to achieve a sufficiently relaxed position is the opposite problem to that of too much tension. The 'collapsed' rider lacks the poised alertness needed to be ready to make the continual tiny adjustments to the aids which keep a horse balanced and moving correctly.

Canter work

The minimum of lateral work is enough for the horse at this stage, and as soon as Emma has got the idea, David sends her on into canter. Every rider who is genuinely trying to improve will find that a change to a faster pace automatically heralds a new range of problems, nearly all resulting from his/her increase in tension. David's first comments are, 'Keep quiet in the saddle, don't keep working your body – relax it!' As the mare picks up speed, he instructs, 'Do a little circle if that happens, and settle her. You don't need to do a lot – just a little bit of voice will encourage her without the need for leg aids.'

A good rider on an explosive horse like this, he points out, can sit and appear to do absolutely nothing, yet have the horse going sweetly and make it look easy. 'Then when you get on it, you find it's a nutcase!'

'Your hands have gone solid,' he warns Emma, having given her a few moments to sort herself out. 'You can nearly have that draw-rein between just two fingers if you like, like a piece of silk, if you keep them active.' The mare begins to respond as Emma remembers to play on the reins, but her position is still tense, tending to crouch over the horse, with locked arms.

'Sit up and enjoy it,' says David. 'Use your wrists gently. I can't hear you talking to her.'

'I just did,' says Emma.

'What did you say?'

'I said "Good girl".'

'There, it works, you see!' The mare begins to go better as Emma sits more upright and relaxed, using her hands as instructed.

One of the dangers of draw-reins and the reason they are so often criticised is that less experienced riders are frequently much too heavy with their hands, thus pulling the horse into an unnaturally overbent position, whilst failing to train the horse also to use its back and hindquarters. David is encouraging Emma to be light with her hands, using the draw-reins as no more than gentle encouragement to the mare to lower her head to the point where she can work in a balanced way, remaining under control, and where she can begin to build up the correct muscle development for a showjumping horse.

Containing the buzzy one

Now David gives a few gentle reminders of some of the things they have done so far. 'Move her head one way, then the other, Emma. Watch your legs don't touch her. You've got to be very, very quiet with her.'

There is improvement, but it is not consistent. 'Do you feel yourself tightening up on her sometimes?' David asks, then explains how Emma can maintain control, once she has it. 'If she starts going too fast, bring her round in a tighter circle, shortening the draw-rein. If you shorten the draw-reins on a circle, you get her head lower. Then as you straighten up, give the rein to her – and hopefully her head will stay down.'

At the first attempt, the mare quickens again. 'If she starts to get strong, be quick. Make a really determined effort to steady her up, then the second she comes back, let her go on again. Stay relaxed with your arms and reins.' This time the mare responds. 'Right, pat her on the neck, now, while you are cantering. Talk to her. Just stay at that pace, but let her have her head. There – now she's changed down a gear or two, hasn't she?'

The success of the strategy depends upon the rider being both relaxed and quick to anticipate the horse's movements. Just as a tense horse is resistant to the rider's commands, a tense rider, his muscles locked, cannot feel his horse's movement nor give gentle and precise aids. This sensitive mare is not altogether settled, but Emma is now able to make her corrections quickly and accurately – and David is equally quick to praise.

The canter work is repeated on the opposite rein, which proves to be the mare's stiffer side and therefore more difficult; but Emma has now understood how to use the draw-reins as an aid and how to relax and control her own body so she can use them effectively and gently, so the work is more successful.

A student who had a similar problem the previous day has been watching the lesson. 'I think what you said about the short sharp check is important,' he suggests. 'Because yesterday, when you told me to relax and give the rein, my horse was just galloping off.'

"You have to take her back first, and *then* give the rein,' David explains.

'But I took her back and kept her there too long?'

'Yes, then you had her fighting you, and when you *did* give, she was off, because you had wound her up from behind, too. So your check must be positive and determined, but it must not be rough. And as soon as she responds, you give back. That's the way it works.' David grins, 'You made your own problems – I try to prevent them!'

Towards collection

The next step of the mare's schooling on the flat, he explains, will be to start pushing her hindquarters up to achieve more collection, the beginning of 'coiling up the spring' that provides the power to lift the show jumper off the floor. This obviously will not be easy with such a sensitive, quick horse, and it will take a rider with a good seat, skilful hands and quick reactions – some of the aspects that make up the quality of having a good 'feel' for riding – to be successful. The mare could do well with the right rider, but she is an excellent example of the type of horse which would be a disaster for an inexperienced or insensitive rider.

The mare's sharpness and tendency to rush appear again when she is given a jumping lesson. David sets up a simple cross with a placing pole and lets Emma ride it in her own way. The mare stands off and makes a big jump, while Emma makes a big effort to go with her.

'Don't get too anxious, you're building up to a big crescendo there,' he warns, as Emma comes round again. 'Let the horse do the jumping – she's too heavy for you! Come in a little bit closer next time, it will help you. Can you use the pole as a bit of a brake?'

The second jump is a little better, but Emma is still attacking it from too far back. 'I had to go on that stride, didn't I?' she asks.

'No, you could have put in another one. But even on that stride, you could stay more relaxed. Work the horse back, going down the school and get her to relax more, bearing in mind that that big stride winds her up.'

This problem of coming in too fast and standing off too far is a common one for inexperienced horses and riders. Someone asks, 'Would it help to come with a shorter approach?'

'Yes, it would, because you would have more chance of having a shorter stride. The horse's hocks would be underneath it a bit

'Emma is going much too fast, the horse has stood back and everything is happening too quickly.'

 (*Opposite above*) 'This is her "Pony Club" imitation! She is trying too hard and doing too much.'

(*Opposite below*) 'Emma is looking at me, the trainer, instead of through her horse's ears at where she is going.'

(*Above*) 'Here, over a less demanding obstacle, the picture is improving. Emma has quite a good position but is just a little too tense. Posing for photos is never easy!'

more on the turn, and it is actually quite difficult to see a good stride from such a long way away. But it's Emma's choice where she's coming from, not mine.'

The next jump is better, but then Emma tries to do too much again and David reproves 'We could have had one more stride then, and you gave her a little smack in the teeth when you landed, too.'

'She keeps taking off after the jump,' Emma explains her problem.

'Don't worry about that,' David advises. 'Get your stride short well back and she won't take off as much afterwards. Keep her steady and you'll find it easier.'

Emma makes a concentrated effort to have the mare better balanced and to approach the fence more slowly, with a shorter stride. The jump is better. 'You could still have taken one more stride', David insists.

Emma comes again and this time the striding is right. 'Good girl,' says David. 'You still made a bit of a forward movement, though. Sit quietly and try to make it all a bit easier and relaxed.'

Encouraged by the noticeable improvement, Emma is enthusiastic to get it right – and does. 'That was better!' she says confidently.

David converts the fence to a vertical. 'Stay relaxed and look for your stride. But don't look for a big one, look for a fiddly one and let the mare do the jumping,' he reminds her.

Emma follows instructions and achieves an acceptable result. 'You might criticise and say it wasn't very good,' is David's verdict. 'But it wasn't that bad either, because you kept her calm and she stayed calm. You would improve on that, far more easily than you would on a big stride. For this level it was all right, because the whole thing was together after the fence, as well as before.'

David's teaching technique

The jumping lesson showed quite clearly that David's aim with any exercise, with each horse, is to improve one aspect, or overcome a particular problem, and not to achieve perfection in one attempt. Everything takes time to become established, and to avoid confusion each step is given careful attention. Sometimes, especially working with his own top level horses, David will know exactly what problem he wants to work on. More often, however, the scope and progress of the lesson will depend upon how a particular horse and its rider perform on the day concerned, and the level or difficulty of the work will vary accordingly. Even good, experienced riders can have bad days or have faults that need to be ironed out, whilst promising horses who have been working well can suddenly suffer an off-day, or throw up a new problem.

Each lesson must therefore be tailored to the individual horse, rider and circumstances at the time, and it is part of David's skill to be able to assess these factors and be as flexible in his approach as necessary. Frequently, tack will be changed in the middle of a lesson, if he thinks that will have a beneficial effect or help overcome a problem. The situations that arise are so specific to each individual case, with so many variables involved, that it is impossible to lay down strict technical rules as to how to cope with them.

David's way of describing what he tries to achieve is that 'You have a picture in your mind of how the horse and rider should look, then you make the adjustments you need to achieve that picture.' Since horses are not machines, he is also always ready to vary his techniques, and if one thing does not work, he will try something else. David's ultimate object in teaching is to help a rider to achieve a correct result so that he or she will experience how it *feels* to ride and jump successfully, and to be able to recreate that feeling later.

'This sequence demonstrates the use of a placing pole on the approach to a fence. The student, Jenny, has a nice style, which is quite pleasing to the eye.'

teaching the showjumping rider

Rider position and technique

What should the rider's position be over a fence? 'Remember that the horse's front legs have got to clear the pole first, so sit in the middle until he has got the front end up – you don't want to be too far forward. Go with the horse over the top of the fence, bend your body so you give, but not too much with your arms. Then the horse will feel less pressure on his back and his back can come up. Over the top, the horse should have freedom.'

Styles of riding and types of horse differ in different parts of the world. 'German horses have to be trained, because they tend not to think for themselves. Then they have to be ridden by pushing the right buttons. If you try to ride a British horse to the button and he decides to do something else, you've got a problem. But British riders don't usually ride that way, it is more a combination of horse and rider.

'The Americans have more Thoroughbreds, and they are supertrained – everything is technical and done by the book, but I think as a result sometimes they lose flair. You have to be able to use your own eye.'

Emma's next jump is not so good. The mare, having begun to understand what is required of her, comes in quietly to the jump on a short stride, but Emma sees a bigger one and goes for it. She acknowledges her fault ruefully. 'It was quite nice of the mare, wasn't it?' says David. 'But if you hadn't done a couple of nice jumps before, she would have gone on the big one. Remember, that closer stride is always safer.'

'But not at a show?' queries another student.

'Within reason,' David replies. 'If you always go on those big ones, you'll be in trouble.'

Finally he indicates a parallel fence, already set up in the school, as the mare has jumped the vertical several times and is losing concentration. The fence is almost immediately after a corner and the first jump is not good. 'Hold on' instructs David. 'The jump is actually on an awful stride there.' And he moves it further along the school, to give the novice horse more room. 'There are so many different aspects to all this, when you get right down to it, which we all take totally for granted,' he observes.

In the next jump Emma anticipates the bigger fence by letting the mare stand off again. 'No! We'll have one more stride please, next time. You are making trouble for yourself when you stand back like that. Just keep her steady, sit quiet and relaxed.'

Emma collects the mare together, and David encourages her on the approach. 'There is no width there at all, you can treat it like a vertical. Stay like that a bit longer. Steady, steady, back, back, back . . . That's better! Did that feel better?' he wants to know.

'Yes much,' agrees Emma, now looking eagerly towards the fence for another go.

'You can't stop her once she gets going,' David observes with a grin. He talks her firmly through one more successful jump, and then advises that that is enough for the day.

'Can you see the difference?' he asks. 'When she gets that big stride, she's off, but with the short one, she lands and she stays with you.'

'And you can feel her,' adds Emma.

'Yes,' says David. 'It's easy when you get it right.'

David adjusts Jenny's foot position so that her toe is in and heel down. 'How many times have I told my children that?!' Then he encourages Jenny to straighten her back and make her position more effective (inset).

6
SHOWS AND COMPETITION

Every horse and of course every rider at some point make their competition debut. The experience should not be one of nail-biting anxiety – the aim should be for both to enjoy themselves, getting round and building up their confidence. Nowadays, the starting-point for most people is indoors, at the multitude of evening sessions at riding centres all over the country. 'In years gone by, you had a six-month break in the winter so you started out in the spring, but nowadays it is probably easier to go to a little indoor show, because the horse does not have so many distractions,' David points out.

'To start off a four-year-old you can do a course 1ft 6in to 2ft – the important thing is to get the horse round. I remember the very first time I took Sportsman out was at Hereford, when the first fence wasn't a foot high – and he stopped! I couldn't believe it – my super novice! Then he went round giving everything about two feet!'

Jumping indoors

Although indoor jumping is so popular, David warns against overdoing it with the young, inexperienced horse. 'As far as the horse is concerned, you've got the school walls to hold him in, he can't run anywhere, there are no distractions from outside and the walls do make it easier to turn – although you have more distance problems and you can't re-organise a horse much indoors, except on the corners. And there is nothing worse than indoor jumping on novices, with long distances – three long strides into a fence teaches him nothing.

'I think indoor jumping is fine for the ordinary person to go to and it's a nice initial thing for the young horse, but he doesn't want to do too much indoor jumping early on. He wants to go three or four times, then go outside; it's outside you get the experience. I've known of horses making Grade A in the winter and then they are greenhorns when they go outside.'

This temptation to overdo the indoor jumping with a promising young horse is a strong one for the amateur rider, but should be resisted if the horse is to have a successful long-term career.

How do you tell if your young horse has had enough and what should you do about it? 'I would read the signs,' says David. 'If he is getting lethargic and has no enthusiasm, if his ears are clamping back and the spark has

'As a young horse, Showman's balance here is not perfect. Shocked into a sharp turn, everything looks a little ragged. However, we did come second!'

gone out of him, then he's done too much. I would send him hacking.

'If he's getting sick of jumping, give him a couple of weeks off, though be careful of just turning him out in the field, as more horses are injured galloping around the field than in show jumping.

'I'm sure people overdo it with young horses. I think three-year-old jumping is the worst thing that could happen to them – their joints are just not ready for the concussion or to take the weight. I can't think of many good three-year-olds that have been good at twelve or fourteen, I really can't. And the younger he is, the more care you should take as to the ground you jump him on. A four-year-old jumping on rock-hard ground will probably jump quite well, although the damage you are doing is unbelievable. Surprisingly, youngsters do jump well on the hard. It is only when they have got sore feet and a bit more experience that they say "no" – and those that don't want to come down, won't go up! So you must bear in mind the horse's mental attitude.'

Over the past fifteen years an international indoor circuit has developed for the top show jumpers, so that there is no longer an 'off' season; riders therefore have to juggle with resting their horses, and having them ready for the major competitions throughout the year. It is abroad that the big money prizes are to be had – with the exception of the Horse of the Year Show and Olympia, the major shows – so David prefers to turn his Grade A jumpers out for their holiday at Christmas, and concentrate on the novices in the yard through the winter.

'The economics of running indoor jumping mean you need a large number of riders and small prize money, which you get in novice classes. The little centres cannot afford to put on more than £25 or £30 classes.'

In fact the huge amount of enthusiasm for the sport is clearly shown by the number of riders who do enter the lowest classes and unaffiliated competitions. 'I went to a local show the other day to present prizes. The class started at 7pm and I thought we would present the prizes at about 8.15pm – we actually presented them just before 11 o'clock! There were 180 people there and none of them jumped over two feet high!

Affiliated jumping

David is concerned at the number of people who show jump at unaffiliated level, as opposed to joining the BSJA (British Show Jumping Association), and is anxious that the Association should encourage these riders to join. 'I believe that anyone who goes show jumping should be a member of our Association. I don't mean they should have to pay the same subscriptions as I do. There should be a very low level of subscription now, to make sure that everyone has a go, even if that membership only allowed them up to Newcomers level. Of course, one of the advantages is that as a member you do get insurance.' (Today, no one is wise to compete in equestrian sport without third-party insurance.)

The current cost of joining may be the negative factor for many people, but the idea of affiliated jumping itself, as the official, organised arm of the sport, should not be. 'We do have low classes, but people have this great mental barrier about going from unaffiliated to affiliated, which is ridiculous. They should be able to go and enjoy it. They would have the advantage of our jumps, indoor arenas which are properly looked after, trained judges and a consistent standard.'

So far as the cost is concerned, David would like the Association to come up with a low cost, practical scheme to attract the new member. 'We have to get a package that excites them. We have to sell our membership.'

When David first entered the sport, the organisation was much simpler than it is today. 'You did 14.2hh jumping as a junior, then Grade C and Opens all round Wales. Then Sir Harry [Llewellyn] introduced the

Foxhunter class to try to get the farmer to come show jumping – that was the idea.

'Trevor Jenks used to take the jumps round Wales, and he had a set of rustic fences for the Foxhunter class that used to be about 3ft 6in high, maybe even 3ft 3in, just one step down from Grade C. It was a lovely class in those days. You would have the regional finals around the country, with the final at Wembley, and it used to cover basically the first year of the jumping horse – there wouldn't be a horse in it over six years old. But it has gone haywire now, and you get horses there who have won a class at Aachen! They can actually be qualified for next year's final before they take part in this year's regional!

'I would like to see it as maybe the only class that the top riders could start winning money in. There is no need for us to go in Newcomers classes, they should be left to the amateurs – or we could jump, but not go to the regionals or finals. And I'd like to see the Foxhunter go back to what it was meant to be – for six-year-olds.'

The Foxhunter competition may have got away from the class as it was originally intended, but there are many affiliated novice classes and qualifiers which enable a rider to follow a progressive programme. Newly registered horses go into Grade C and are upgraded when they have won a specified amount of prize money, currently over £799; Grade B covers horses with winnings from £800 to £1,799; and Grade A winnings of £1,800 plus. An owner can upgrade a Grade C horse by declaration, before its winnings have reached the limit; but once upgraded, a horse cannot revert to Grade C level competitions.

By far the majority of privately owned and ridden show-jumping horses remain in Grade C, competing at a level which is enjoyable for the amateur rider who is unlikely to work full-time with horses, but enjoys riding as a leisure activity. An increasing number of people from non-horsey backgrounds are taking up riding as a recreation in middle age and competing alongside the enthusiastic teenagers, and David is keen to encourage them to learn. 'Their horses may never be of a high standard, but they do it for their own en-

joyment and why not? I did a course the other day in Ireland and there was a 45-year-old banker jumping who had only been riding for two years, but was thoroughly enjoying it!'

The rider who show jumps as a hobby, however, should be aware of the role of the BSJA at international level. It is from here that the sport evolves and progresses, with new ideas and improvements filtering down to provide the best possible standard of training and competitions at grass roots level. 'Colonel Ansell always said that the health of the sport depends on its international success,' David reflects.

The importance of good ground

For the amateur rider, limited in his choice of shows, planning a competition programme can be difficult. In summer, if shows do not water their arenas, the ground can be rock-hard and very off-putting to the inexperienced horse, as well as damaging to its limbs. 'Clay ground is horrible when it's wet,' says David. 'Good grass is obviously the best surface. It's a good thing to spike the ground to get the water six to nine inches down – you must make the roots grow down for their water instead of up, to get a good surface. Sandy soil with good turf, well watered, is the best.

'Aachen has wonderful ground, well prepared, with nice thick turf. And the Polo Ground at Barcelona used to be wonderful, lovely thick grass with a good mat, peculiar to that area.

An early competition outside: 'Meynell Park jumping very well.'

'If the ground is hard in the summer try to choose the shows that are watering their ground. The novice rider who has no choice other than the Saturday afternoon gymkhana where they wouldn't think of watering has a problem, but it is surprising what you can do if there is a stream nearby. Put 10,000 gallons out in the morning, and it takes the sting out of the ground.'

If the ground is really bad, however, for the horse's sake the rider might be well advised to miss a jump-off, or even not go to the show at all, although he points out 'At a lower level the horse is not going up so high – you can go quietly down to a 3ft 9in or 4ft fence and just pop over. When they get bigger, you have to have a little more force in it.'

For an indoor surface David prefers ordinary topsoil, kept damp to stop the dust and with some shavings mixed in, to any of the proprietary surfaces. 'Some of these are tough on their joints when the jumping is big, whereas on grass a horse has a bit of give when he hits the ground. An artificial surface can be like jumping onto glue.

'If you have an indoor school with good topsoil what you must do once or twice a year is put a mole plough through it about eighteen inches down and a yard apart, just to shatter the pad underneath – not so much that you turn it over, as you would never be able to ride on it, but just enough to break up the subsoil and keep the top three inches loose. Then you roll it, and off you go again.'

(*Right*) Checking the fickleness of the planks: 'Horses don't respect them quite as much as the poles.'

(*Below*) Walking a course. David starts to measure the distance of a combination.

 # Walking the course

Once you have chosen your show, entered your class and arrived at the showground, how should you set about preparing for the competition and riding the course?

Walking the course is an art and everyone works out their own way of doing it. Obviously you must know your own stride length and how this equates to your particular horse's stride. David has explained his method of measuring combinations in Chapter 4 (see page 53) and the need to take the spread of the various elements into account, but there are other aspects to consider. For example, is a fence sited near something which is likely to make a horse spook, such as a water-jump with the sun shining off it, or a fluttering flag? How is the ground riding, and

what is the take-off and landing like for each fence?

Is the fence on a slope, where it would be better to approach to the higher side, rather than the centre; or is the approach downhill, where it will be more difficult to keep the horse balanced and you will need to steady him? How will you ride the corners, to make sure that the horse remains supple with his hocks underneath him? And will you remember where the first fence is, when you ride into the ring?

This latter point, says David, is the hardest thing to remember about finding your way around the course, especially if the track is designed on two circles. 'You have to make sure you get on the right circle!'

The importance of warming up

Warming up is always essential, whether for schooling or performance. When preparing to go into the ring, however, it must be done with concentration and forethought – it is not just a case of trotting a few circles and popping a couple of practice jumps.

'Get the horse out and walk him round. Let him have a look at things and a trot round. If you have plenty of room, pick your own bit of ground somewhere, trot a few circles either way, do a little half-pass to get his back end moving, and a bit of shoulder-in.

'Extend him for a few strides and then bring him back, to see if he will come back – and if I'm too frightened to do that, it means I haven't got him schooled very well. Often I don't do it because I don't want to do it, and that is a great weakness and a flaw. Event riders tend to gallop on too much without coming back; show jumpers are inclined to be the other way, and have them too much together without opening them up.

'It's no good letting the horse extend and then having him all unbalanced and out of control. When I teach people, I tell them the actual halt is as important as anything. If you want them to stop, they should stop.

'My father was superb at doing this. He would get on a horse and work him, without draw reins or anything, and I've seen him work a horse that was a bit hot for three hours so he could extend him and bring him back. And after all, it's what you want to do in the ring at the end of the day, and unless you can extend and come back, you might as well forget it – that is what sorting out a stride is all about.

'Here is a nice story to illustrate the last point, one which I tell everyone: your job is to find the stride for the horse, to get him on the right spot at the right time. It is just like a little boy jumping off a wall with his Dad down below to catch him. He jumps down and Dad catches him – it's no problem at all, and he will keep jumping off the wall. But if Dad drops him once, and you try and get that kid to jump off the wall again – he won't do it, will he? Well, it's the same if you fluff the horse's stride up – in the end he will refuse to jump.'

Paying too little attention to schooling and having the horse under control is undoubtedly a major contribution to stopping and napping. 'That is why green horses are so difficult to ride. In fact sometimes an experienced rider can't do much more with a green horse than a novice rider can, because it doesn't really listen to anything.'

Once the horse is suppled up with these flatwork exercises, it is time to try a practice fence or two. 'He should be cantering forward nicely, with a light contact, not pulling your arms out. Then trot down to a cross once or twice, to see if he is listening and paying attention. If that is all right, progress to a vertical a couple of feet high and build it up, perhaps to 4ft 6in high, depending on your class. Then you go back to a parallel and build that up, and I always finish with a big vertical.

'I've done that for about thirty years. The Americans always start with a dinky little parallel and there is a certain amount of credibility in that, as a horse has to make a shape over a parallel.

'I always ride him a little bit deeper than I would in the ring so that he is paying attention and listening; and I always put my last vertical higher than anything in the ring, if I can, so that I've stretched everything that has got to stretch. That said, if you're in a puissance competition you obviously don't jump a 7ft fence outside; but I jump a decent vertical.

'Also, you need to get your timing right so that you are not doing all this half-an-hour too early – then off you go, into the ring.'

(*Opposite above*) 'This photograph clearly shows how easily a horse can catch himself with the jumping studs in his shoes.'

(*Opposite below*) 'Warming up Showman over the cross-poles establishes a good shape before going into the ring to tackle the bigger fences.'

(*Overleaf*) 'It is very important to establish a good foundation. Here, Showman shows his progress in the sport, making a good job of jumping an oxer in a B & C class.'

shows and competition

'Meynell Park jumping a vertical on the turn at Hickstead.'

Technique in the ring

Nearly everyone suffers from nervousness before a class, but as David points out, that is not going to help and you must find a way around the problem. 'You are probably always a little bit up-tight before a big occasion, but nerves are not going to help you at all; so ultimately, when you go through into that ring you must forget them, get on with it, and just worry about how the horse is going. If you and the horse have got it right, your aim is to jump the jumps and that is enough to worry about without impressing the crowd as well.

'If you are last to go and you might blow the cup for Britain – well, if that's going to happen, it's going to happen. *Your* job is for you and your horse to jump the jumps.

'Whilst you warm up outside, you should be remembering what you will have to do in the ring. If the third fence is a couple of oxers, you need to make sure the horse really *is* warmed up outside. On the other hand, if the first seven fences are quite nice, you don't actually have to do so much outside and can warm up as you go round. As long as the horse is paying attention and listening to you, there is no point in wearing him out outside.

'If in doubt about a stride, I'll put an extra one in. Having said that, when walking the course, I'll measure a lot of the distances for academic sake, then see how they actually work out when I'm in the ring. My brain has got to be ice-cold, so that if I'm doing my job properly, I can tell you where every leg was on every stride.'

This emphasises that in order to cope with situations that arise in the ring, it is vital to combine theoretical knowledge and practical adaptability; things don't always go according to plan, and the rider must be able to ride intuitively and adapt almost instantaneously to the changing situation.

'You must have a certain amount of flexibility,' says David. 'I remember once I walked an eight-stride distance to a triple bar; when we came to jump I landed pretty simply and began to count 1,2,3,4, 1,2,3,4 – and I had the biggest crash under the sun, finished up on the floor amongst the lot, and vowed I would never do it again.

'At the end of the day, your eye should be your judge. I think the British have been brought up that way – you can have all the theory in the world, but it is your own eye that counts.

'The Americans have their equitation classes for which they have to work to a system, whereas traditionally we have been brought up through hunting and riding all our lives, and doing our own thing. However, we can all be polished and made better.'

The event riders that David teaches have a particular problem in that after the gallop of the cross country they must collect their horses together so they put in more strides and jump with sufficient spring and impulsion to be neat and accurate.

'Their sport is going to have to get sharper at our discipline in my view. In doing the cross country the day before, the horse's stride has gone from twelve to fourteen foot, and they have to get it back again to get it right in the show jumping. But eventers *en masse* seem to have this mental block towards show jumping – they all tell me they can't see a stride, but that is rubbish because they can see a stride perfectly well when they go across country – what they mean is that they know when they are wrong, but they don't know what to do about it. But if they shorten their horse's stride up, it gets easier. The only stride you can see when you are too long, is forward; you can't take one back.

'Over a five-stride distance, you should be able to come in five strides, or in six, and if you do your job correctly, in six even strides.'

Of course the problem is not always one of inadequate riding. Some horses are simply not talented enough to jump above a certain level, and even if they are physically capable, the mental ability might be missing and the horse builds no confidence in the rider. In that situation, says David, 'You do your best, but you don't know whether it is right or wrong. There is an enormous area of grey'.

Riding the course

Once you are in the ring, all your preparatory work is put to the test and various factors all come into the equation: your horse's strengths and weaknesses, the way the course builder has built the course, the ground conditions and the time allowed, your riding ability and your partnership with the horse.

'A triple bar is not that important in isolation, but in relation to the next fence it could be very significant. For example, if it is followed by three strides to a big vertical, it is going to ride differently than if it was the last fence – you've got to get your balance back to tackle the vertical.

'Outdoors or indoors however, the most important thing is rhythm.'

Developing and maintaining a good rhythm in the ring depends upon having the horse under absolute control, and the need for this is why show-jumping riders are sometimes criticised for their methods of schooling. Of course in a perfect world, horses would always go on the bit without being overbent and with their hocks engaged and backs rounded up. Sadly the world is far from perfect, and schooling is often seen to exaggerate the optimum in the attempt to achieve it, in the same way that the evading or unschooled horse reacts by going in the opposite direction.

'You are never going to get it all quite right, but it is important that you have gone through the motions of making every muscle move: to simplify it – if the horse can't turn left, for example, that's tough; but if he turns left but won't just shorten on the left turn, it means you can't use that bit extra to shorten or lengthen him, and you know you can't; so he comes round, for instance, with his head looking the wrong way and it all makes life difficult. You are lengthening the odds against getting it right at the fence.'

This is a point not considered by the 'gadget' critics. 'John Whitaker can't ride a horse with his head stuck out in the air, so if he can't do it, what chance has anyone else

got? John, Michael and Nick have their horses under control. Why? To get the odds in their favour.

'You don't want to overdo it, but if you can put the horse's head where you want it, it will come back again – even if you work it down to the floor, it doesn't get stuck there, you know!'

Of course having said that, the rider should be totally aware of what is happening to the horse underneath him, of why he is riding in a certain way and what he is hoping to achieve. And it is no use having the horse's nose behind the vertical if his hocks are way out behind him – optimum control can only be achieved from working both ends of the horse.

COMPETITION TIPS

1. Work out a method of walking the course that works for you.

2. Remember where the first fence is!

3. When warming up, work in on the flat, doing circles, then ask your horse to extend and come back to you – make sure he is under control.

4. David starts his practice fences low with a cross, then a vertical, and builds up to a parallel, finishing with a vertical that is a bit higher than anything in the ring.

5. Relate your warm-up to the type of course – how soon will you meet the difficult fences?

6. Nerves won't help – concentrate on the horse and the jumps.

7. If in doubt about a stride, put in an extra one.

8. Theory is all very well, but in the end, it is your own eye that is your judge.

9. Indoors or out, the most important thing is rhythm.

No one, however talented, gets it right all the time. 'You do take a gamble now and again and it doesn't work,' David admits. 'I did something at Millstreet last year in the Derby. The one that went before I got on my horse did something funny at the bank that frightened the daylights out of me. I've never had trouble with the bank, but I got this idea that I would ride Lofty without a martingale and would fiddle him round and have him backing off everything. I can't remember the theory behind it now. Anyway, I did this totally against everything I've ever done before, convinced it was going to work, and it was the biggest disaster under the sun! I couldn't hold him, couldn't do anything, and I'd had five down by the eighth fence.

'I have come to the conclusion that when I come down a bank I feel I am not more than forty per cent in control of the situation. When I'm approaching any other type of combination, I would expect to be ninety-eight per cent in control, so in the circumstances I retired.'

The incident, although a disaster, clearly shows David's famous ability to stay cool and calm whatever is happening. To have the presence of mind to sum up his situation so precisely whilst actually riding, requires a really detached and professional attitude.

'It totally altered my thinking. I had made the biggest mess I have ever made of it, changing everything at the last minute – though so often I had come up trumps with it, that sort of shock treatment, altering something.

'The idea is to try to knock a bad habit on the head, but the trouble is that when something works for one horse, you are inclined to do the same with all of them – like with bits that become very fashionable for a short time.'

The year's programme

As the season progresses, everything is geared towards the bigger and more important competitions, when winning is important. Earlier on, however, the important factor is to get the horses going well, sharpen up their jumping and prepare them for the work ahead. At this time a good performance and a win or a placing is a bonus; but there is much more happening besides, as David assesses how each horse has come back from his winter break, also the progress of the novices, and evaluates their strengths and weaknesses, and tries to find solutions to problems.

The first outdoor show of David's year is usually the first of the season held at his home on the Wales and the West showground in mid-April. The Grade A horses will have completed their early fittening and schooling work and will be ready to start jumping, and the novices will be facing the switch from indoor to outdoor jumping.

The Wales and the West provides a considerable service to show jumping in the region, and is one of the biggest showjumping centres in the country, with four multi-day shows each year and five arenas in operation, covering everything from open competition to 12.2hh ponies, all affiliated to the BSJA. It runs young riders' international events and training sessions, and for the first show of the year, the seven-acre parking field is crammed full of horseboxes.

For David's horses, however, it makes for a relaxed beginning to the season – they have only to walk a few yards from their stables to reach the show-ground.

David aims to jump them all each day of the show, principally to give them a chance to get back in the swing of jumping and to have a schooling round. 'I have never really got horses to give an absolutely tip-top performance on day one. They have to be jumping fit and there is nothing like the ring to sort out a few problems, or to show them up – and then you've got to go home and work on them.'

If they go clear, the Grade As will often be withdrawn before the jump-off, if David feels they are not ready for it. 'The situation changes from day to day.'

shows and competition

According to David, by the 1993 season Showman had had a fair bit of experience. He is an example of the situation where an owner can declare a horse upgraded so it can jump in higher level competitions before it has actually won sufficient prize money to be automatically upgraded. Showman's low prize money winnings does not reflect a lack of ability, but the fact that he did not pursue an intensive campaign in his formative years. 'I don't get to many shows where he can do Grade C jumping,' David explains. 'I hope he comes good. He can do some lovely things, and he has a big heart and a lot of ability when he wants to show it.'

David's aim with a good young horse is to give him experience to bring him on, rather than to campaign through each level. Quite apart from the fact that his own time to bring on novices is limited, he does not believe in over-jumping young horses. For example, Showman's career began with some small indoor shows, progressing to outdoors and then success in Gleneagles, Foxhunter and Grade C qualifiers. Inevitably at some stage problems occur in bringing on the youngster, and in Showman's case he failed to progress through the regional Grade C and Foxhunter stages. Careful schooling saw him through the setback and he gained more experience abroad, as there was room for him on the lorry. By the end of that season he had begun to look like a horse who might reach the top, and after his winter break and warming-up shows the plan was that he should join the Grade As in their continental travels through the following summer.

Once a horse is upgraded to Grade B, he does not necessarily stay there long if he is going well. 'When I bought St James and won enough to get to Grade B, he stayed there exactly seventeen days, by which time he had won enough in A and B classes to move up to Grade A.'

7
TACK AND EQUIPMENT

The tack used by show-jumping riders is one of the most emotive and controversial subjects in equestrian sport. Those who express outrage are often as uninformed and misguided as those at the other extreme who compensate for lack of skill by tying down the horse with every imaginable gadget devised to 'aid' correct training, and then subjecting the unfortunate animal to pain and fear through gross misuse of the equipment concerned.

Any piece of horse tack – even a snaffle bridle – can be used to abuse the horse, in the wrong hands. However, this does not mean that equipment designed for specialist purposes is automatically a bad thing in itself. David's tack room is equipped with some powerful pieces of tack, whether referred to as 'schooling aids' or 'gadgets', and he is the first to admit that he will cheerfully use anything he thinks necessary to achieve the desired results.

However, each piece of equipment has its own specific purpose, and its own place in the training of any horse for which it might be used. And no equipment is ever used in a way to cause distress to any horse, nor as a means of force. As David continually points out, show jumping depends upon a partnership between horse and rider, with the horse willingly co-operating. Specialist equipment can encourage that co-operation by helping the horse to understand what is required and encouraging him to use his body in the necessary way; but it can never force him to *jump*, and anyone who tries to use force as a method of training is doomed to failure.

The snaffle bridle

The standard tack for a horse being worked at home in David's yard comprises a snaffle bridle with a thick, plain, single-jointed bit, usually with loose rings rather than an eggbut, a flash noseband, a running or sometimes a standing martingale and draw-reins. The saddle will be an ordinary jumping saddle with a numnah for protection, fitted with webbing girths, and the horse will wear tendon boots on the front legs, plus overreach boots if he is jumping.

'I like to work a horse in a snaffle bridle if I can, because it's soft. You want to get him bending his head without doing it too much from his mouth. All I'm looking for is that arch from his nose to his tail.

'If the horse has a really soft mouth, you might use a rubber bit, but it usually isn't long before he has progressed out of that.'

A loose-ringed bit is preferred to an eggbut in most cases, because it allows more play of the bit in the horse's mouth, encouraging the horse to salivate and giving the rider a more sensitive feel through the reins. (An eggbut avoids any risk of the bit pinching the corners of the horse's mouth, in less careful hands.)

(*Below*) Feedback in his basic tack for flatwork: snaffle bridle, flash noseband, draw-reins, jumping saddle and working bandages. As he is not jumping, there is no martingale.

(*Right*) The saddle in place, with the 'banjo'-shaped foam underneath to ease jarring on the horse's back.

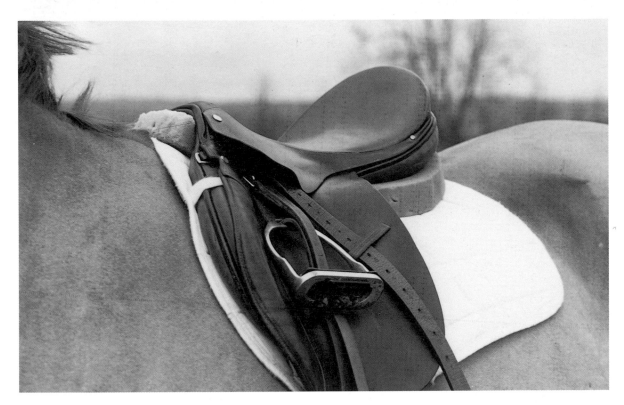

Nosebands and martingales

Some of the tack used as a matter of course is there more to prevent problems from occurring in the first place, than to correct a problem which has already happened. A young horse, for example, will frequently try to evade the bit by opening his mouth, and at worst even learning to put his tongue over the bit. Fitting a flash noseband correctly at the start discourages this tendency because it prevents the horse opening his mouth.

Similarly a young, novice horse will often throw his head up in the air as an easy means of escaping the rider's hands via the reins, and a martingale will prevent him from getting his head up beyond the point where the rider loses all control. There is a safety aspect here, too, since a young horse which suddenly finds himself free of the rider's restraining hands may very easily take off at speed and perhaps panic, becoming a danger to himself and others.

A correctly fitted working bridle with flash noseband.

In this picture the running martingale is slightly too short.

The running martingale is most frequently used in the jumping arena and in David's view should be fitted so the rings are in line with the line of the reins from the horse's mouth to the rider's hands. Fitted in this way, the running martingale only comes into effect when the horse raises his head above the point where he loses balance; it has no effect whatsoever as long as he is working correctly and obediently. Over a fence it allows the horse the flexibility to stretch his neck and head, without interfering with his action.

The running martingale acts directly on the rein, however, with a downward resisting pull on the bit. Provided the horse reacts by giving to the action of the martingale, this does no harm and with an older horse, in a competition, it really serves as a reminder to keep his head correctly positioned to respond to his rider's aids, thus giving the rider more immediate control. A novice horse, however, might resent the pull on the reins when he raises his head, and could well resist against the action of the martingale and its pull on his mouth which is, says David, the very part you want to keep sensitive and soft. For this reason, he prefers to use a standing martingale on a young, inexperienced horse which is inclined to be difficult in this way.

The standing martingale acts on the nose, leaving the mouth alone, and the horse will usually instinctively lower his head against pressure on his nose rather than resisting it. If the standing martingale is fitted too long, however – which many people are inclined to do – the horse can lean on it and eventually build up muscle against it; so it must be short enough to discourage him from that.

'Its surprising how short you can have it as long as you are not jumping enormous fences,' David points out. 'When I first won the King George V Cup, I had a standing martingale on Sunsalve. Generally I look at a horse and see where it is needed. You can hold the martingale in a certain place where a horse can't resist it, and then he gives to it – and that is my rule of thumb for fitting it.' The problem of the horse building up a resistance is a risk with any piece of equipment which is designed to control him, so correct fitting is always essential.

Some people would object to the idea of putting a martingale on as a matter of course, but David maintains: 'You don't want his head in the air, and even if it doesn't do a lot of good, it also won't do a lot of harm. When the horse first does anything wrong, his head goes up – unless he's going to buck, and then it goes right down – so I always like to have some means of controlling the head.'

Tongue-over-bit evasion

Another problem that sometimes has to be solved is when a horse puts his tongue over the bit. 'You can't ride a horse with his tongue over the bit, you lose all feeling in the reins.' Remedies vary, from tying the bit upwards to the noseband, to tying the tongue down to the lower jaw. The former works in a similar way to the rubber noseband often seen on Thoroughbred racehorses, where a single strap runs down the front of the face and then divides, each strap passing to the bit-ring on each side. David might use a simplified version of this idea on a pony, but for horses, his preferred solution is a simple tongue strap. This is a webbing strap with an adjustable loop through which the tongue passes, which is then buckled under the jaw. Great care must be taken not to fit it too tightly, as this would risk cutting off the circulation – something which could happen very quickly, with dire results. 'It doesn't have to be that tight, just enough so that he can't get his tongue back out.

'Mr Ross was the most athletic horse with his tongue I ever came across,' David recalls. 'I got this amazing bit and I was going to beat him at all costs. Well, he couldn't get his tongue over it, but he couldn't jump either – what a wonderful solution!

'It was much too fierce and he was thinking

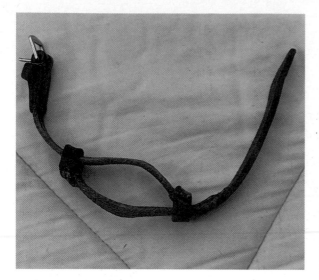

'My theory is that a horse who puts his tongue over the bit could at first have been reacting to pain somewhere, but then, little by little, it became a habit. It's like a person with a hole in a tooth – you keep putting your tongue in it, and it hurts, you know you shouldn't do it, but you continue to do it and it's maddening! It takes over your concentration.'

(*Left*) The adjustable tongue strap, and (*right*) the 'monster' bit which Mr Ross couldn't get his tongue over – but in which he wouldn't do anything else, either!

about the bit more than about his jumping. We did use it for exercising him, but at the end of the day, it was better to put a tongue strap on – then you know exactly where his tongue is, and away you go.

The double bridle

For more advanced schooling, David favours the double bridle. 'When I've got a horse nice and soft in a snaffle, with his head down and supple, then I want to get him off his forehand a bit and build up more compression from behind. I don't want to hold him down there forcibly on the draw-reins, so I switch to a double bridle.'

He looks for a 'happy medium' in the type of curb bit he uses, with a low ported mouthpiece, the cheeks neither too long nor too short, and he prefers the sliding cheek to the fixed type. 'I like to have a bit of play in the bit – when it's solid there's no give; and I've never found a high port of any use.'

There are several ways of holding the reins when using a double bridle; the modern fashion is to cross them so that the snaffle rein runs between the little finger and the third

finger, with the curb rein between the second and third fingers. The theory of this is that the snaffle rein has the most immediate contact and the curb takes secondary effect. However, David was taught by his father to keep the reins parallel, so that when rotating the wrists, the curb rein comes into play immediately. 'I've never understood why the modern style is to cross the reins – why shouldn't they run parallel? By using just a little bit of curb and asking him to give to it, I can get the horse nice and short, with his hocks right underneath him. But you have to be very, very sensitive with the curb, or the horse can reject it completely.'

This view is typical of David's attitude to the use of equipment – if you are going to use something, use it in the way that will be most effective, but use it competently, precisely,

A correctly fitted double bridle. However, David prefers a curb bit with sliding rather than fixed cheeks.

and with understanding and sensitivity. He sees no point in playing safe with the curb rein by holding it inside the snaffle rein – but then his seat on a horse is so independently secure and relaxed that he is never in the situation, frequently seen in cases of bad riding, of trying to keep his balance by hanging on to the reins. He is so experienced that he does not need the safeguards for the horse that riding manuals recommend to the less skilled.

'I do love a double bridle, and actually the foreign riders are using them more now, too. I started back in about 1970 with Sportsman and Philco, riding them in a double bridle in the morning, with a draw-rein on the snaffle bit, so you could have their heads in the right place and also have the lightness of the curb. It's interesting that even the Germans are using them now, for working their horses, and actually like them.'

The pelham

David is also fond of the pelham, especially for ponies. 'I used to ride all my ponies in pelhams, because Father used to believe that a snaffle was too soft. If you have the hands to ride in a pelham, you have that bit more control, although it's no good being mutton-fisted with a pelham.

'Now, we've got little 12.2hh ponies and Matthew is riding in a pelham – he has a lot more control than with a snaffle, and is a lot happier. He's riding with one rein and a D coupling and the whole system is a lot sweeter.'

The rider must remain constantly aware of the amount of pressure he may expect to exert on a horse's mouth with any particular bit, in order to obtain and keep the horse's co-operation. It is fundamental to success and not easy to do. Both the choice of bit and the way it is used, play equally important roles.

'Imagine having an E-type Jaguar and driving it on ice, with heavy boots on, in bottom gear. You need total finesse to get the car to grip without spinning the wheels and going out of control. In those conditions, very few mistakes are forgiven and it is the same with the horse.

'In the show-ring, when you want these quick turns, you put a lot more pressure on the horse than you would under normal circumstances, and you are asking the horse to forgive you for pressurising him. You do a quick move and you may think you are doing it nicely, but I bet most of the time you are a bit rough.

'The bottom line is that in training, you are trying to build up a relationship with your horse, so that he will accept it if you are more demanding and hard on him in the ring.'

Bits and pieces

In recent years the use of gag bits for show jumping has become more popular, whether the conventional gag used with two reins, or the sliding American type; and there are always new varieties of bit on the market, most recently those with soft mouthpieces made of a sort of plastic. David has never been particularly successful with or enamoured of the gag bit.

'Some people are very successful with them, but my mind doesn't relate to a gag bit, though it might work sometimes. It's all a matter of trial and error and what your horse will accept. Very often, and especially for a difficult horse, I will use a rotation of bits: I will use one for so long, then change to another, then another, and so recycle them.

'I will use different bits for schooling and for the show-ring. And I might warm a horse up in one bit, then change to another for the competition.' If necessary, David will even change the bit between rounds in a competi-

Countryman's jumping bit.

keener again. It's all a vicious circle. He's very difficult from that point of view, and I've never found the right bit for him yet.'

Bitless bridles, or hackamores, also had a huge surge of popularity following the great success of Eddie Macken with Boomerang. 'They play their part,' David agrees. 'Although I've never had great success with them and they do vary an awful lot. They are not all as severe as they are claimed to be – how can the one with the spur strap under the chin be severe? But if you have one with a chain under the jaw, that's different. There are all sorts – Paul Schockemöhle makes his own. But it's easy to follow the fashion – you find a bit that you quite like, that's in fashion, and if you're not careful, you'll have six of them. Then its magic will disappear and you will be back to confusion again.

'I've got another bit here that we call the elevator bit, which is a snaffle with long fixed cheekpieces above and below the mouthpiece. That will actually stop a train. I won the Grand Prix at Olympia a couple of times using it on Philco, but I used to use it with two reins – one on the bottom and the other in the middle for steering. You can't steer on the bottom rein when you are going against the clock and want to make a quick turn.'

 The elevator bit, sometimes worn by Philco.

tion. 'We've done that many times, though it hasn't always worked out!'

For the past four or five years Countryman has done his competition jumping in a long-cheeked snaffle with copper rollers in the mouthpiece. 'Lannegan is much more difficult,' says David. 'He gets ambitious half-way round the course and is too keen. You get him quietened down, then maybe have a couple of jump-offs where you have to go against the clock, and you've made him

Saddles

It is vital when saddling a show-jumping horse that the saddle does not interfere with his spine, so a well fitting saddle with a clear channel through the gullet along the spine is essential. The forces involved in a big horse taking off, stretching over a fence and landing on the other side are tremendous, so the saddle must help the rider to sit well and minimise the effect of jarring to the horse's back. Jumping saddles are usually based on a spring tree, rather than a rigid one, for this reason, and the flaps are cut well forward, with the stirrup bar set slightly further forward than in a general purpose saddle; this allows the rider to get his weight forward over a fence and stay with the horse's centre of

gravity. The seat is relatively deep, but not exaggeratedly so as in some dressage saddles, and a knee roll is incorporated to give the rider more security; there is sometimes a thigh roll, the original purpose of which was to help keep the girths in position.

David uses a variety of saddles, according to how they fit his horses, but has no particular favourite at the moment. 'I used to have a leather Toptani, the first Toptani I ever had, which was a beauty to sit on, but I could never get another one made like it,' he says regretfully.

'I think the older you get, the more difficult it is to find a saddle you fit into well. Your stirrup length gets shorter, and you lose your

The 'banjo'-shaped foam in position over the numnah, ready for the saddle.

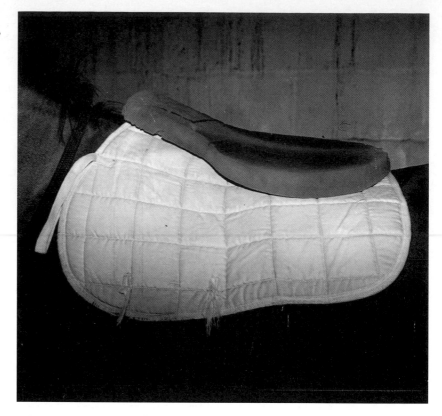

grip and stay on more by balance. I'm sure I'm not so stuck in the saddle as I used to be.

'It's really a question of choice, what you get used to and what you like. When I went to America, I found I could sit on a Hermes saddle quite well when I got used to it. On the other hand, there is nothing nicer than to put your knee into something and feel really locked in.

'The most important thing is that it fits the horse. It can really hurt a horse if it comes low on the withers and the rider is a lump of weight in an ill-fitting saddle. We also use a numnah underneath to give a bit of protection, and on Phoenix Park, who was getting a bit older and dipped in the back, we used what we call a "banjo", which is a thick piece of foam rubber shaped like a banjo. It fits under the saddle, narrower in front and spreading out wider under the seat, and helps lift the saddle up a bit.'

Girths come in many designs and materials, but David sticks to a traditional method of girthing, using double webbing girths. 'Father always believed in quite a tight saddle for jumping, on the grounds that it is bad enough for the rider to be slopping about, let alone the saddle as well. But you never pull the girths up tight to start with. You always want a couple of holes left after you have mounted, then wait a couple of minutes and pull them up again.'

At the last minute before going into the ring, a surcingle is put on over the saddle. 'I always use a surcingle, for two reasons – it keeps the saddle flaps down, and it is there just in case of an emergency if the straps or girths break.'

Standard stirrups are used, with a rubber grip so that it isn't so easy to lose them. 'New stirrup leathers are inclined to keep stretching,' David points out. 'I put half-holes in them, because as they stretch you keep thinking you're riding too long. And I must say, the older you get the more finicky you get. There's nothing worse than a leather that feels too long just as you're going into the ring, because you feel awful, you can't sit properly in the saddle and everything goes to pieces. Over the years my stirrups have got shorter, and very often you'll see me just nipping up half a hole – it must be only about a quarter of an inch, if you think about it, but it just gives you that extra bit of security.'

Protective equipment

Jumping strenuously and turning sharply mean that the show-jumping horse may be quite likely to injure himself, and various items of protective equipment are used.

The protruding studs usually screwed into the shoes to help prevent the horse from slipping, can cut his chest if he lifts his front legs high under his body when jumping, so a wide leather guard can be fitted as a sort of body armour. Open-fronted tendon boots are standard equipment for the forelegs, the big tendons at the back of the cannons being the most vulnerable to damage from the hind feet striking forwards. Overreach boots are also used, and here again David is a traditionalist and prefers the pull-on type.

He also believes in bandaging, rather than using just tendon boots, if a horse has any indication of weakness or a leg problem. 'I think it gives a lot more support. It's the same as a human being – if you are playing any sport and have got a weak arm or thigh, you bandage it to give it support, don't you? We've always believed in that.'

In general protection is not required on the hind legs unless a horse has a tendency to brush or to knock into himself, in which case fetlock or brushing boots will be used.

Various schooling devices

With the exception of draw-reins (for their use, see page 43) and martingales, other schooling aids are used infrequently and only when occasion demands. If a horse is to be lunged, a Chambon will usually be fitted to encourage him to work in the required outline, with his head low. The Chambon is another frequently criticised item of tack but, like everything else, it is only harmful if used incorrectly, and correctly used, achieves a thoroughly beneficial effect.

It should be remembered that no equipment is capable of producing the desired results from a horse *in itself* – it is what the trainer does with the equipment that counts. Also, most items are not intended to force the horse into a correct position, but to discourage it from avoiding a correct position; and a green or young horse is only encouraged to take up the desired position by degrees, as his muscles strengthen and develop. The Chambon, for example, is always fitted loosely at first, and only tightened gradually as the horse accepts it and becomes more balanced and supple. 'Besides, as soon as a horse "gives" to the Chambon, its effect is relaxed,' David points out. He never loses sight of the fact that a horse will not co-operate if he is uncomfortable.

Instead of coming from the girth and passing between the front legs to the bit, draw-reins can be fitted as side-reins, and David will use this method occasionally if a horse has developed the habit of 'poking his nose out'. He also has a piece of tack specially designed for schooling certain horses who once in a while decide to lean against all the usual aids and refuse to lower their heads: this works by exerting pressure on the poll and by keeping the head too low to resist. 'Lannegan went through a patch where his head would come up and he went really stiff on me and wouldn't give, but that worked for him. It doesn't tie the nose in – if the horse's nose is tucked into his chest you can't ride him either.'

David has a serious word of warning for anyone tempted to use this or any other unconventional equipment without either experience in its use or help from an experienced person. 'For example, with this particular device, you must be very careful that the horse doesn't panic and rear up, because they can easily flip over backwards – it's unbeliev-

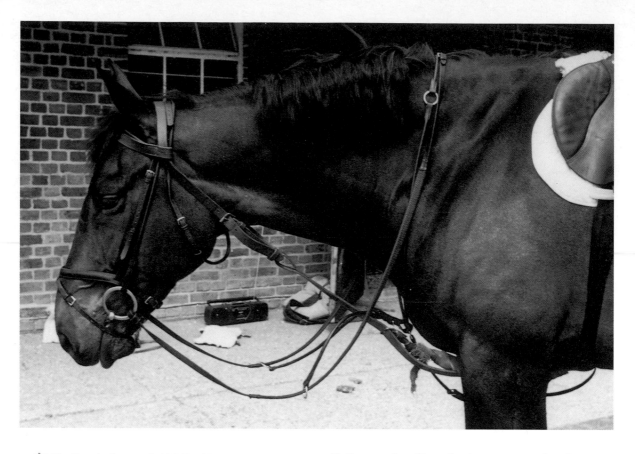

 The 'headcollar strap' which David occasionally uses to encourage a horse to lower its head, when more conventional methods are unsuccessful. David stresses that such equipment should be used only with extreme caution and with help by someone experienced in its use. Even a quiet horse can panic if it doesn't understand what is happening, and can seriously damage itself or its handler.

able how easily they can do that. Any new piece of equipment must be fitted very carefully because the quietest horse can panic, and then you are in a dangerous situation.'

Another point that should be made is that all these schooling devices are used only temporarily, to achieve a particular effect, and as soon as the horse has learned the intended lesson the item of equipment is removed. It is an aid to achieve a purpose, *not* a crutch to depend upon. They are certainly useful tools to help with the job in hand, but they are not, in any sense, the key to any particular 'David Broome method' or 'mystique'. That lies in the skill of David's own hands, seat and eyes.

Artificial aids: whips and spurs

The final so-called 'artificial aids' to be considered are the whip and spurs. 'I don't often carry a whip, because I'm always losing them,' admits David. 'And most of my horses are sharp enough not to need a stick in the ring – it's just another thing to handle and another thing to lose. It's bad enough looking after my hat when I take it off – wondering where I've put it, or where the groom has put it – without having a stick which everyone else seems to want to pick up as well!'

However, there is a place for the whip when schooling a horse, David feels. 'With a lot of horses a dressage whip can be very useful when you are working on the flat. Sometimes you don't want to be kicking the horse on, and a little flip with the schooling whip will get him up into the bridle. But hopefully, you won't need a whip in the ring.'

Spurs are another matter, and David always wears them, regardless of the horse, or whether he is jumping in a competition or schooling at home. The type of spur varies, however. 'I've got some very good little short ones, then I've some medium ones that I've used for about fifteen years. For one little "donkey" horse I've got, I actually bought some spurs with wheels on and that has bucked up his ideas no end – so it's different spurs for different horses, really.'

Spurs, of course, are another emotive subject. David's head girl, Emma Storey, says 'David always wears them because he maintains you never know when you are going to need them. Like he says, "I can wear them and *not* use them".' And this is the crux of the matter: to have the riding ability to be sufficiently in control of your legs that you can bring the spurs to bear only when you wish. Also, of course, spurs should be brought into play only with gentle pressure, and never with a prodding or jabbing action. The wearing of spurs gives even more emphasis to David's insistence that the rider's normal position should be with his heels down and his toes in. A toe pointing outwards and a grip-

With David's toe pointing correctly forward, the spurs do not come into contact unless and until he wishes to use them. His foot is positioned in precisely the right place to give aids just behind the girth.

ping calf give rise to continual involuntary use of the spur, and a rider who has not mastered a sufficiently independent seat with control over his leg movements, should not wear spurs.

 # The riding hat

Finally, in the interests of safety, all show-jumping riders are now encouraged to wear riding hats of an approved standard. Like many who grew up before the days of safety-conscious riding, David dislikes the modern safety helmets. He acknowledges the need for head protection and the importance of setting an example to young riders and children, and wears a hat with an integral safety harness when required. The rule regarding a safety harness has not yet been enforced on the international jumping scene, but David believes this is only a matter of time, even though head injuries from accidents in the jumping arena are comparatively few.

He still has two well fitting hats without safety harnesses which he wears from time to

time, but his main objection to the modern helmets is not from the safety point of view but from that of appearance. 'For cross-country riding and the race-riding jockey, the crash helmet kind of fits with the rest of the dress. But our modern hats have done nothing for our image. It was discussed when the rule first came in, but the manufacturers have done nothing to make the new hat look the part. Some of these hats are so bulky – someone is going to have to come up with a special design one day.'

Despite his personal objections, David is very aware of the need for every safety precaution when riding, and prefers anyone schooling the horses at home to wear a suitable hat.

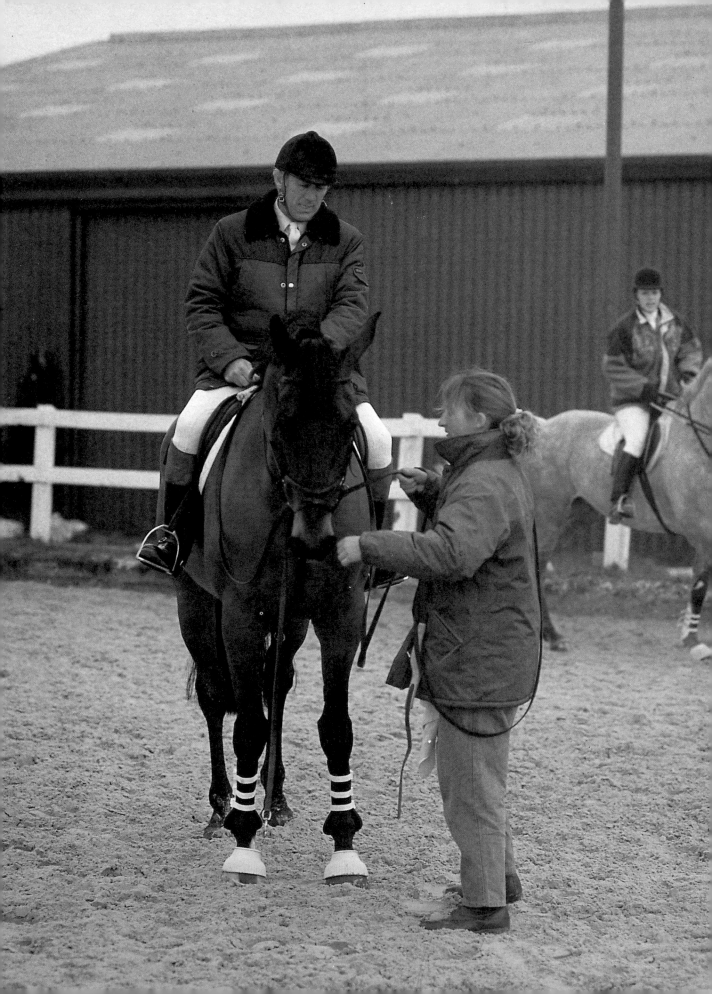

8
DAVID'S GRADE A HORSES

One after the other the three Grade A horses are brought back into work in March. They will have enjoyed two months complete holiday, having been turned out after the pre-Christmas International Show Jumping Championships at Olympia to spend their days at leisure in the fields, roughed off and protected from the wet and cold in New Zealand rugs. At night they will have been brought in to their evening feed and stables, though each horse has his individual quirks of temperament and Lannegan, for one, is never keen to come in from the field once he is on holiday.

This break is essential for horses competing so intensively at such a high level. It gives muscles, joints and ligaments a chance to rest and to repair any minor strains and sprains, and just as importantly, it gives the horses a period of mental relaxation and refreshment, without the stress of travelling or the pressure and tension of the show-ring. When they come back in, they should be eager and ready to go back to work. Much as they need a rest, horses which have become accustomed to a busy life, with lots of attention, can soon become bored with nothing to do. The thirteen-year-old Countryman will have been hacked out, during his break, to keep him 'ticking over' now that he is getting older.

Buying the current Grade As

Countryman, Lannegan and Feedback all arrived at David's yard around the same time, and in the early days he rated Feedback the most promising. Countryman, known at home as Dennis, was purchased in Ireland – like many of David's horses – from Frank Kernan (the father of show jumper James Kernan) after six months of negotiation by David's long-time sponsor and friend, Sir Phil Harris. Sir Phil has played a very prominent part in the last twenty years of David's career, and he and Lady Harris are also now the main owners of Michael Whitaker's string of horses. After years of travelling the world and jumping in the most prestigious competitions, Countryman is still a somewhat highly strung individual and very much a 'blood' horse, which makes keeping him calm and settled no easy matter. 'But he's a lovely rhythmic horse to

ride, with tremendous ability,' says David.

The next arrival was also Irish. 'I went to Millstreet Show and was watching the four-year-old class and thinking about buying the winner, when an Irishman came up to me and said 'Would you buy a horse that will take you back to the top?'

'Well, I'd heard this kind of thing before, but we said we would try the horse. It was a great rangy thing and the greenest novice you ever saw, but with a huge jump and a nice attitude. Eventually we bought it, and that was Lannegan – a big, raw novice but with a heart of gold and an enormous jump.'

The chestnut Feedback had continental credentials. 'I've bought several horses in Switzerland and I was there to look at some others, when this horse was brought in and I quite liked the way he jumped.

'He was the best novice of the three – if I wanted to win a novice class I took Feedback. He's very cute and has a lot of ability, but he

Warming up Lannegan before a competition, David exchanges views with Nick Skelton.

David's grade A horses

doesn't have a big heart to go with it. He has the scope if he wants to show it, yet he can make 4ft seem like Becher's Brook!

'He came through the novice ranks and was in several finals at Wembley and could have won any of them, but he ended up winning nothing. I don't know how I've managed to keep him – but he's gone a lot better in the last two years.'

To categorise the three horses: Countryman has jumped the big courses, just missing an individual bronze medal at the Seoul Olympics; tall Lannegan – known at home as Lofty – is the dependable, calm and willing, consistent money-winner, though not quite so easy to ride over the biggest courses; and

Feedback is the 'speed horse', neat, careful, with ample scope and a cool head but less than brave, but who can be put under pressure against the clock – something which not all horses will readily accept. Therefore each has an essential role to play.

They are cared for primarily by Emma Storey, who travels with them during the season, stays with them when they are abroad, and refers to them lovingly and proprietorially in her no-nonsense fashion as 'my horses'. She is responsible for their feeding, their grooming and turnout, tack and exercise and their health and well-being in every way, and she has been David's travelling head groom for several years.

Early work

Work begins with walking out around the local lanes and roads to harden off the horses' legs and get them used to work again. Trotting is introduced gradually after the first three weeks, and some lungeing to start suppling up joints and muscles without the weight of a rider. Most of this early work will be done by Emma, with David on hand to discuss any problems. When they are ready to start schooling, with a show in mind, David

takes over some of the flatwork and does what little jump schooling he thinks necessary for the first show, which is quite likely to be the Wales and West's own first summer show at Mount Ballan. The idea is to ease back into the competition season with the minimum of pressure on the horses. How they perform at their first show will pinpoint any difficulties that need to be sorted out, and help David plan their early schedules.

Routine at a show

The horses' routine at home has already been mentioned (see Chapter 2, page 30); when they go to a show, however, it changes and Emma is kept busy all day. The timetable depends upon whether the show is indoors or outdoors, whether it is summer or winter and when the horses are due to jump. The Olympia Christmas Show, for example, the most popular of the whole year with riders, grooms and public alike, goes on late into the evening; but then the first jumping class is not until after lunch, to start off the matinée performance.

The atmosphere at Olympia is festive, and

not only the arena but also the stables are brightened up with colourful decorations. The area taken over by David's sister Liz Edgar, her husband Ted and daughter Marie is particularly resplendent, with the newly relaunched colours of their team sponsor – the biggest in British show jumping. David's corner is more modestly arrayed, with traditional tinsel and coloured balls – though Countryman's stable is denuded. 'Dennis has destroyed them,' Emma explains, retrieving a coloured ball from the shavings. Either the superstar is not entering into the spirit of

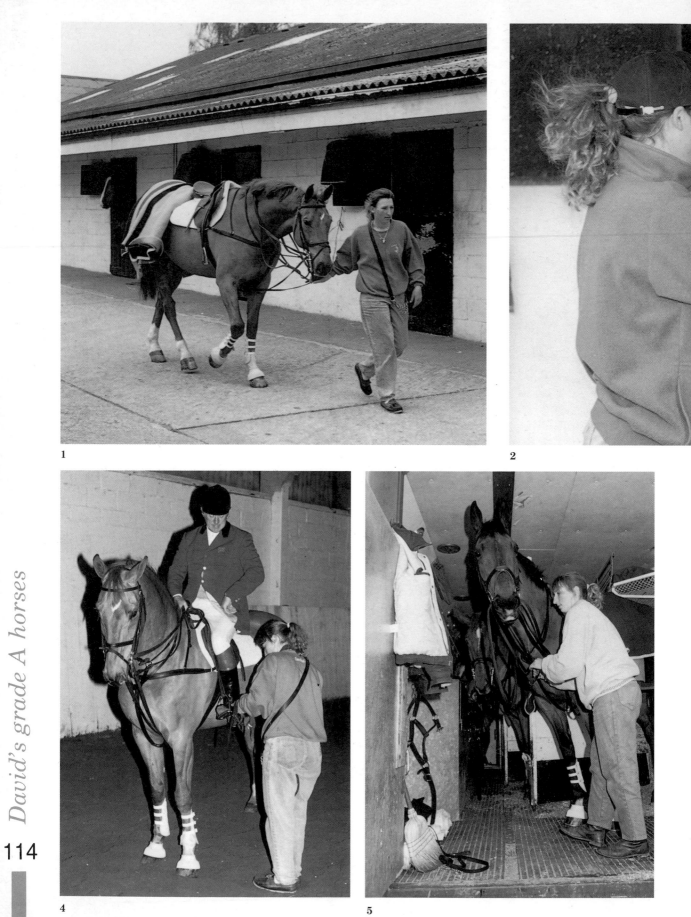

114

1

2

4

5

3

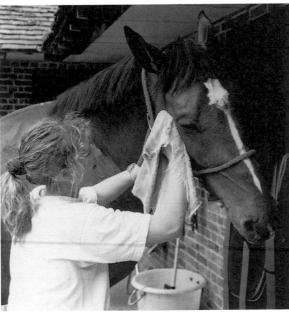

6

7

'A groom's work is never done!'

1 Emma leads out Feedback for work.
2 Painting the stable door with 'anti-chew'.
3 Putting up a practice fence for David and Countryman.
4 Changing David's spurs.
5 Tacking up Showman in the lorry, for a local competition.
6 A towel down for Lannegan.
7 Fitting jumping studs.

Christmas, or he thought it was a new way of keeping himself entertained!

For once, since the horses may not be finished for the night until midnight, there is no need to be up early in the morning, so their first feed will be at about 8am. For a show like Olympia, with four classes on the programme each day, David will have all three horses in contention, if possible, so there is plenty to do.

Straw is usually available at the stables, but Emma's charges are bedded on shavings, and in one case, on paper, so she brings their bedding from home. Mucking out and laying down the horses' day beds is the next job on the agenda. Water buckets, fastened to the stable wall with a spring clip, are filled and likewise haynets, then each horse's rugs are removed and shaken out and he is groomed, ready for his morning exercise. At shows, grooming is even more important than at home, since (except at international competitions where security is a priority and the stables are closed to the public) the horses and stables will be on public view and high standards are maintained. Before work the horses are basically just tidied up: dust and stable stains are removed, manes and tails brushed out – Emma has a baby's hairbrush for the short, pulled manes which avoids breaking the hair – and feet always picked out just before the horse leaves the stable, so that bedding isn't dropped all over the floor outside. Keeping the stable area tidy saves work!

After work, and after the horse's jumping class, more thorough grooming is done. Each horse is untacked and a sweat rug thrown over his quarters, and he is led outside to a hosing area provided by the show management where Emma shampoos and hoses down his legs to get rid of sweat and dirt from the arena or working area surface. Back inside, the horse is left to cool off.

Indoor stables at the big shows are usually very warm, so a light rug may be all that is needed – though everything is flexible, depending upon the situation. Once cool, the horse is groomed all over his body with a plastic curry comb to get rid of sweat, then with a stiff brush, which amounts to a body massage. His face, eyes, nose and muzzle are cleaned with a damp sponge. At a summer show on a warm day he would be sponged off with a hot cloth and body brushed. On a really hot day Emma might hose him down completely.

Once Emma is happy that the horse is clean and comfortable, he will be given his haynet and left to relax, while she gets on with the next job, either cleaning the tack just taken off, or preparing the next horse for David to ride. With three horses to be exercised and all competing, each with different tack and different needs, she has to be constantly alert. Each horse must be tacked up ready for David to ride when he wants it in the morning – often one is led out as the previous one is brought back.

Before a competition the horse is got ready for David to warm up, and Emma accompanies him to the practice ring, with a kitbag containing anything that might be needed, and the horse's rug. She legs David up, watches him ride and adjusts the practice fences for him as required. Before David is called, the tack is checked, the draw-reins removed if the horse has been wearing them, and then Emma follows as far as the ringside to watch 'her' horse jump. At a big show like Olympia the atmosphere can become very tense, and the grooms are as caught up in their horses' successes or failures as much as anyone. Success, of course, makes the show memorable; but equally disappointment, which is inevitably more frequent, must be shouldered philosophically if anyone is to survive in such a competitive world.

David himself remains cool and calm under pressure – another facet of his character for which he is noted. A student once asked him how one should cope with the pressure and distraction of the crowd at a big show. 'Forget the pressure,' said David. 'Keep your mind clear and don't worry about it. Think about the horse and the jumps – that is enough to worry about!'

After David's round, Emma throws the rug over the horse's quarters as he rides out of the arena and walks him for a few minutes to let him relax. David usually returns to watch the rest of the class. If the horse has gone clear and there is a jump-off, he is kept tacked up and ready, and depending upon how long he has to wait, will either be kept moving to prevent him stiffening up, or brought back out to warm up at the appropriate time.

After one class Emma is asked by a steward to remove Countryman's boots for checking. This random checking is a welfare measure, designed to protect horses from the rare, unscrupulous rider tempted to use illegal methods in the attempt to make a horse jump more carefully. It acts as a deterrent, more than anything, and no one is exempted from it – even a rider known to look after his horses as well as David does.

Tack is cleaned each time it is used and Emma fits this in between all her other duties. A spare stable is used as a tack-room, where everything is kept hung up or folded and stored away neatly and tidily – you can't afford to be untidy when you are likely to need something in a hurry. Emma has devised a complete range of portable racks, hooks, hangers and boxes, so that wherever she goes with her horses, she can set up her equipment and follow a set routine, making life easier for her and for David.

The horses have their second feed at lunchtime, their third at about 5pm after the afternoon performance, and a fourth in the evening, after the last horse has finished jumping.

The horses are fed a basic diet of chop with competition nuts or coarse mix, and Emma will vary the amounts of concentrates according to how the horse is going and the work it is expected to do. They are often given HorseHage as well as hay, or sometimes instead of hay, particularly if they are spending a long time indoors, or are especially susceptible to dust. Being packed in compact, plastic-covered bales, HorseHage is easier and less messy than hay to transport.

The problem of air polluted with dust, spores and ammonia fumes is ever-present, and at a five-day indoor show such as Olympia, the horses are at even greater risk than usual, going straight from stuffy indoor stables to an indoor arena and back again. There is no outdoor exercising area here either, so between all her other tasks, Emma makes a point of leading each horse out for a walk around the car park for ten minutes at least once a day.

It isn't all work, however. On the final morning of the show there is a little publicised groom's jumping competition, when the behind-the-scenes carers have an opportunity to show what they can do. Emma is a previous winner, riding the 'speed horse', Feedback.

Travelling in Britain

Once the season starts in earnest, Emma and her horses are seldom at home. Early in the summer, the British national competitions at horse and agricultural shows all over the country get under way, with competitions such as the Area International Trials (AITs), qualifiers for the King George V Gold Cup at the Royal International Horse Show; David has won this no fewer than six times! There are prestige shows – Royal Windsor in May and the Royal Show in July, as well as the Royal International at Hickstead. Before long the international competitions are also in full swing, with the round of Nations Cup

A wall-mounted fan helps provide ventilation in the lorry.

events when David is a regular member of the British team, as well as plenty of other international shows all over Europe, or even America.

Packing up the lorry for a long trip is an art in itself – there isn't much space, but there is a considerable amount of equipment, from buckets to bandages and bedding, from sweat sheets and saddles to feed, forage and the mucking-out skip. Nothing must be forgotten – even Matthew's bicycle if he is included in the trip, for getting around the show-ground. David's elder son, James, does ride but is now more involved with his studies at school; Matthew, however, is an enthusiastic rider and his pony will often accompany David's horses to British summer shows, where junior jumping is on the programme. 'He is very observant,' says David. 'He watches every class and will soon tell me if I have done something wrong!'

Home comforts! A peek inside sister Liz Edgar's lorry.

Douglas Bunn's yard at Hickstead.

Countryman at the Seoul Olympics in 1988.

Lannegan

Lannegan, the same age as his stablemate, is '. . . as honest as the day, with an awful lot of ability. All he tries to do is win me money,' says David. And Lannegan has done his share of that, winning the King George V Cup, Leading Show Jumper of the Year, and the Millstreet Derby, to name a few. 'He's a wonderful Derby horse as he never spooks at anything – nothing ever bothers him.'

As a young horse he proved very good, almost winning the National Grade C Championship – but for the last fence down – and at eight years old he finished the highest placed qualified horse competing at Hamburg. Like all horses, he has his ups and downs and David is currently trying to overcome a tendency for him to become too keen in the ring.

'He's wonderful in the practice arena and over the first five or six jumps, but then he builds himself up and gets stronger and stronger. He doesn't stay cool in the head, and when you have to start putting the pressure on it just winds him up quicker. I can do anything with him over just one fence or a grid, but I think all I can do at home to try and get over this problem is have a course of seven or eight fences up and practise jumping him over sixteen fences at a time, so he gets happier with the idea of jumping courses.

'He's very big and his back end is much lower than his withers, although he's very powerful. He's a bit of a freak, really, and is awkward to turn – his co-ordination is not that wonderful making quick turns. Whether that confuses him and makes him get tense, I don't know.

'He had a bad year in 1992 – he tweaked a muscle at Dublin and was never really right again until the end of the season, so his main claim to fame then was a third in the Aachen Grand Prix. On that occasion John [Whitaker] was in the ring before me, when the heavens opened. I was sheltering under a tree when they called me and it was still pouring. I looked at the sky and saw it wasn't going to get any better and they were still calling me, so I cantered in.

'It was sheeting down, but I saluted and started off. Lannegan's ears went back, and by the time I was over the third fence my saddle had gone like a piece of soap and I couldn't grip. I jumped a big double, then there were three more fences and a big combination – a wall, two strides to an oxer and one long stride to another oxer – which two-thirds of the class had stopped at and the rest had down.

'Well, Lannegan, occasionally as a novice could drop a leg in a parallel, so this could be a bad fence for him and I thought, if I have one down before that, I'm coming out. But he was clear and, God bless him, he jumped it beautifully! So I went clear but had a quarter of a time fault because I was concentrating so hard in the rain.

'There were about eight clear rounds and the second round was shorter but bigger and I went clear again. Only Obtibeurs Egano with Jos Lansink and Nick Skelton had double clears and so I finished up third, against the odds with a quarter of a time fault.'

Feedback

When it comes to being competitive against the clock, David is limited in what he can do with Countryman and Lannegan. 'I can only go as fast as they will allow me to ride them,' he acknowledges; but Feedback is the opposite in temperament. David thinks that the fact that Feedback isn't always willing to jump the big fences and his cool head under pressure go together. 'He's ice cold – that's half his problem – but as he doesn't get excited I can ride him as hard as ever I like and be very competitive, and he will go against the clock and still be as careful as a kitten.'

Nevertheless Feedback can show ability when he feels like it – he once cleared 6ft 8in in the Puissance competition at the Dublin Horse Show. 'And that,' says David, 'is a horse who can make four feet seem like a very big jump.'

Feedback may not be the greatest jumper in the world, but he is a reliable campaigner for the numerous speed and novelty competitions at every show.

(*Overleaf*) Lannegan jumping at Calgary in 1991.

9
DAVID'S CAREER: A LOOK BACK

Over the years since he has been at the top of his sport, David Broome has seen many changes. In the early days when David was selected to represent Great Britain, he shared his place on the team with riders such as David Barker and the brilliant lady rider, Pat Smythe. In 1960, when he won his first Olympic bronze medal on Sunsalve, the gold and silver went to the Italian brothers, Raimondo and Piero d'Inzeo. Some great riders have been both team-mates and opponents in the arena: Marion Mould with the incredible little horse, Stroller; his great friend and rival Harvey Smith; the late, extremely talented Caroline Bradley whose early death was such a tragedy for the sport; Derek Ricketts, Malcolm Pyrah, and others. Then there have been great foreign competitors such as Hans Winkler, and Alwin and Paul Schockemöhle.

Riding for the British team

Through all those careers David has remained consistently successful, to the extent that for the past few years he has been the 'fourth corner' of a team which the record books are likely to show as the most talented the world has ever seen. The names 'David, John, Michael and Nick' (referring of course to the Whitaker brothers and Nick Skelton as well as David himself) have become so synonymous with the words 'British team' that other riders despair of ever being chosen, and accusations of nepotism have been levied.

However, the team manager and chef d'équipe Ronnie Massarella has always stood by his own judgement, and the places of the four are by no means sacrosanct. Five riders were selected for the British squad at the Barcelona Olympics in 1992, the fifth being Tim Grubb, nowadays not so well known to British jumping fans as he is based in America. All five went to the Games, but only four would have the opportunity to jump, so a severe disappointment was in store for someone. Not for the first time in his career, the sidelined rider was David.

He had had a fall a week previously in Royan, France; but only Ronnie really knows the reasons for his decision. On that occasion the team won no medals and, as with any stars to whom success sticks like glitter, there was considerable criticism when they failed to deliver.

David, however, has no compunction in supporting his team-mates: 'I've had some wonderful companions, but I've never had three greater than John, Michael and Nick. It has been a privilege to ride with them – it's lovely to be tucked in there with them, and my hardest task has been to carry my own corner.'

The quartet has so much mutual experience now, that working together is second nature – they are always ready to watch each other ride and help with advice and suggestions. 'We do it for team competitions, and when we're abroad, we try to help each other win even in individual classes when we're

also competing against each other! The team is quite unique in that respect.'

Naturally, where the top talents in the world are under pressure at the highest level of competition, there have been disagreements and even rows, when riders and management have differing opinions. However, these are comparatively rare and David fully acknowledges the role of Ronnie Massarella. 'Ronnie has been lucky to have a lot of good riders over the years, but it's never

(*Right*) David's career has taken him all over the world; he is seen here with Captain Mark Phillips, Graham Fletcher and the Princess Royal at the Olympic Games at Seoul.

(*Below*) John Whitaker's great horse, Milton – 'a natural!'

David's career: a look back

British team chef d'équipe Ronnie Massarella with the team which he has led to so many victories: (*left to right*) John Whitaker, Nick Skelton, Michael Whitaker and David Broome.

been his way to overplay his authority. He might rollick us if we've done something stupid, but he's never interfered with our riding, and he's been fantastic in other areas, such as public relations and fostering team spirit.

'He's always kept on good terms with everyone, and will never be bettered from the point of view of team spirit, because he keeps us all happy.'

Of the prestigious shows David has attended all over the world, he remembers many with pleasure; but if pressed, he admits that 'Over the years, I've been to Dublin more times than anyone else and it always seems a bit special to me.

'But it all depends on how well you are going. If you win everything, you've had a great show – you just don't seem to get as wet as everyone else, then!'

The sun has shone on David many times in his life, but two things give him particular pleasure: 'It's lovely when you are abroad, in the team, and they play your anthem. That can bring a tear to your eye, it is very special. You are very lucky to have that moment, I think. Remember, when I was a kid, they used to play the national anthem in the cinema!'

The other special memory is of a record no one else has achieved. 'When I won the King's Cup the last time, I felt very proud that day because I had actually achieved an ambition to win it for the sixth time.

'It was a fairy-tale class, the way it worked out, because I was last to go in the jump-off and everyone else got quicker and quicker. Nick was in the lead and I beat him. It was probably the best of the lot – no, I can't say that because they were all special ones really, but it was one of the most difficult to win.'

The horse he rode on that occasion in 1991 was Lannegan; and it was Lannegan who, in 1992, helped the British team to victory at the home Nations Cup meeting at Hickstead.

Horses and horsemanship

There have been almost as many great horses in David's stable as there have been great rivals in the show-ring, and while the rest of the world may now remember them just as names attached to a list of winnings, to David each one stands out as a unique and individual character. His ability to understand and work not only with the talents but with the failings of every one of them in an objective and sympathetic way, is one thing which has always given him an edge over riders who are less perceptive, patient and determined. From each horse he obtained the best it could give, whilst also appreciating its limitations and knowing when he could not ask more. On the rare occasions when he did have to ask too much – for example, if a British medal hung in the balance – he was always aware of what he was doing, the risk to the horse's future career, and the fact that much careful work might be needed to restore the horse's confidence afterwards. And he never made the mistake of blaming a horse for lack of ability.

'A good rider can get the best out of a horse and make it jump as high as it can,' he points out. 'But not even a good rider can make a horse jump higher than it is capable of doing.'

This deep understanding and care for the welfare of his horses has meant that most have enjoyed long careers at a high level, an achievement for which David has won the respect of both competitors and spectators in the show-jumping world.

Wildfire

The horse that started it all might have been calculated to put anyone off horses – that David was totally undeterred by its evil attitude to all and sundry was perhaps an early indication of a great horseman in the making. Wildfire – a name he lived up to – was purchased by David's father for £60 in 1957 when David was seventeen years old, and was very nearly sold again fairly quickly. David first rode him after returning from the Horse of the Year Show. 'We got him out in the paddock and had a bit of a pop on him. He was the most lovely, magic, bouncy ball I'd ever sat on, just like as if he was on springs.

'He was a blood horse, but he looked nasty, vicious, had his ears clamped back when he jumped, swished his tail, and was a real bad-tempered horse. He hated to be touched around the top of his head, and when you came to put his bridle on, you only got one go at it. In those days the horses were kept in stalls, with a strap around their necks to tie them up. Once he got the strap caught up over the top of his head, and because I was the one

who quite liked him, I was the one who had to go and talk to him until I could undo it.

'Well, we hunted him a lot that winter – people actually hired him to go hunting – then we went to our first show at Glanusk. The third fence was a triple bar, directly away from the collecting ring. I have always had a thing about horses putting in a stop at triple bars and I duly got eliminated.

'Father said to me, "Well, he's got one more chance, then he's off!" The next show we went to was a two-day show at Stow Park, near Cirencester. The first day we had four faults, but he went well. The second day we put him in three classes and he won all three.

'We never looked back.'

By the end of the year Wildfire was the top money-winning horse, with a tally around £1,200. 'That's nothing these days, but when you think there were only three competitions in Britain then with prize money of £100, it means I won a lot of classes for that.'

In the process of gaining this achievement, David and Wildfire came to the attention of

the show-jumping authorities and he was asked to join the team for the Dublin Horse Show. But his father Fred refused to let him go, on the basis that he did not yet have enough experience to represent his country. They did go the following year, however, to Rotterdam. 'Wildfire and another horse won their first class. It was a pair relay and it seemed very important at the time.'

 # Sunsalve

After Wildfire came a horse of which David says 'He was probably the greatest horse I ever rode'. His name was Sunsalve, and he was an English horse from Norfolk, bred by Mr Anderson, whose daughter had already won the Queen's Cup on him.

'He could just do things nothing else could do. He went like a deer and I rode him in a standing martingale so that I could control his head.'

Tellingly, David suggests that his own inexperience in those early days was an advantage when it came to making the most of Sunsalve's peculiarly individual talent. 'I was lucky because I didn't know too much about the game, except what it felt natural to me to do, so I never set out to train him. We had never heard of draw-reins then, but if we had him now, the first thing we would do would be to try to make him bend his neck and back and drop his head and conform. But that never happened and, back then, I could ride him without it.

'My father was brilliant at producing him for me to ride, from feeding and grooming to working him in so as to get his mouth so I could hold him – and that horse could just turn and run and jump from anywhere. He could get underneath a fence and do a Harrier-jet type of jump, too, with a vertical take-off and then landing nearly back legs first – it was most unusual what he could do,

Wildfire jumping at the Royal International Horse Show (*Sport & General*).

Sunsalve, with whom David won his first Olympic medal. David still feels the horse was a cut above any of his other great partners (*O. Cornaz*).

but I rode him in those days with a dash of youth, and that's what he had to have.

'People used to ask if I could ever stop him, and I could have stopped him if I'd really wanted to, but he needed that bit of freedom to explode – and explode he could do!'

Sunsalve gave David his first King George V Gold Cup, but he is mainly remembered as his mount for the 1960 Olympics in Rome, where he won the individual bronze medal.

'The course was big, but he jumped two fantastic rounds there, the second round in both the team and the individual competitions. The combination in the individual competition was almost impossible to jump on one stride and one stride, but *he* did it. The Italians had supposedly been training for six months to jump it in two strides so they could fiddle it,

but there were seventy-two poles broken on that combination on that day. In the first round I was responsible for one of them, because I rode it for two strides and Sunsalve picked up in one, didn't he – and we had an enormous crash. The second round, I made up my mind I was going to try it in one, fail or not, and he just jumped it for fun. It was magic! I can still actually remember the feeling of the jump coming out – whumf! It was just . . . scope unlimited.

'I had the last fence down,' David remembers, telling the story with characteristic regard for the full facts. 'The shadows of the trees were on it and I had been wearing sunglasses for a fortnight, for the first time in my life, and I believe it affected my eyes when I rode without them, because I couldn't see the stride. But it didn't affect the result.'

Sunsalve continued to cover himself and David in glory, going to Aachen the following year and winning the individual gold of the European Championships. 'He carried me round!'

'I was very lucky to have him at that time in my life,' David reflects. 'He used to power his way round, standing back and I don't think anyone has seen anything jump like him since. Milton is a jumping exhibition, but Sunsalve was in a different league in the way he did it. He was the one that could do things that nobody else could do. Mister Softee was a great horse, Philco was a great horse, Milton is a great horse – but none of them could do what he could do.'

Mr Softee

A horse which did a great deal to consolidate David's success in his late twenties was Mr Softee, although the horse did not come to him until he was twelve years old, an age when most show jumpers have reached their peak. 'He was a great horse. He had a lovely character, terrific technique, very quick in front, good behind and he was tremendous, absolutely tremendous under pressure.

'Soon after I had him he broke down, and we had him fired. The next year I think we won the King's Cup, the Victor Ludorum, the Derby and the Leading Jumper of the Year.

The following year I won the European Championships on him, and in 1968 he won the individual bronze medal and was the best horse over the two competitions in the Mexico Olympics. He was the best horse in the team jumping, there were only four rounds jumped within the time limit and he had two of them. The course had obviously been measured short. I will never forget it. There were no clear rounds and I had four faults in both rounds.

Mr Softee gave David two European Championship titles (*Clive Hiles*)

'By that time of his life I made a point of never asking him to jump fences he couldn't make, because he didn't have great length ability – he was very normal in what he could jump in combinations, although he tried his heart out. We went to the Olympics and the fences were enormous – the combination stopped Stroller – and Mr Softee just couldn't make the third part of it, it was physically beyond him. We were four foot short of the back pole and fortunately came down in front of it, so it was safe in its own way.'

The experience could have unsettled many lesser horses, but Mr Softee had more to give yet. In 1969 David again won the European Championships on him, this time on home ground. 'I said then, that the people who saw him win the European Championships at Hickstead were very privileged because he jumped under pressure with speed and concentration. He beat Alwin Schockemöhle with Donald Rex and did it properly. He was absolutely magic, and he was quite an old horse by then.'

Heatwave

An example of a horse which did not quite have superstar quality, but still earned a worthwhile place in David's string, was Heatwave. 'He was a very good national horse. I suppose he could jump within three or four inches of what the top horses could jump, but he just wasn't the big-time horse. He won a tremendous number of good classes for me around the county shows and he was lovely, but he just lacked that little bit of class to take him up into the next league.

'He did have a fantastic show in Rome once, when he won three classes out of three, but it was a struggle for him,' David's ability to acknowledge this, understand the horse, and aim him at the lesser classes for which he was best suited rather than trying to turn him into something he could never be, kept the horse happy and gave him a useful purpose in life. It is not necessarily only with the greatest horses that top riders enjoy their successes.

Beethoven

Another pinnacle of David's career was looming. Douglas Bunn is today best known as the master of Hickstead, the show-jumping ground he has developed in the beautiful Sussex countryside and the home of the Derby, the Nations Cup competitions and, beginning in 1992, the Royal International Horse Show; at the time, Douglas had a horse named Beethoven which he had ridden with considerable success. However, increasing business commitments meant that he no longer had time to do the horse justice, so he passed the ride on to David. 'He was an absolute power-house of a horse in a short space. Talk about the original pocket battleship – he was it! I think he was bred out of a carthorse

mare and he had a bit of a cart mare's attitude to life, but I don't think anything could jump with a better technique than Bootsy. Over a fence he was as neat as a button.'

However, a fortnight before David and Harvey Smith were due to depart for the 1970 World Championships at La Baule, they took their horses to a show in Northumberland. 'One of the features of the ring was an open ditch at the far end with a hedge behind it and a pole behind that. Well, I got eliminated with Bootsy at it, and Harvey got eliminated with Mattie Brown.

Heatwave, jumping at the Wales and the West Show in 1970.

'Talking about it afterwards, we didn't even know why we were going to the World Championships, we seemed to be so under-powered – but then Beethoven pulled out all the stops.'

In the World Championships final competition, the last four riders had to ride each others' horses, and Beethoven put in a good enough performance for David to qualify to take part. David jumped three clear rounds and was left with only Alwin Schockemöhle's Donald Rex to ride. He was the only rider to make a mistake on Donald Rex! The two English horses had faults at the water jump with the foreign riders, so David still took the title with a fence in hand.

'Beethoven could jump, but he was very awkward to ride to a fence in that he would do a little buck on the approach that was guaranteed to put you half a stride out. He played his part with the other riders, except for Harvey, at the water jump, so in a way, he was my secret weapon!'

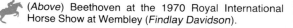

140

(*Above*) Beethoven at the 1970 Royal International Horse Show at Wembley (*Findlay Davidson*).

(*Right*) Manhattan, jumping the wall in the puissance at Dublin, 1979.

Manhattan

A consistently reliable money winner, whom David remembers with rueful affection, is Manhattan. 'Old thickhead! He had all the scope in the world, and won the Puissance at Rotterdam and at Amsterdam three years running. He could pop over 7ft 2in but probably had one of the lowest IQs I have ever come across in a horse.

'It was a shame, because he won a lot of money for me and won a lot of classes, but it could have been three times as many if he had been a thinker.

'The worst moment of my life was the last two fences in the team competition at the Munich Olympics. We were in line for the bronze medal. He hit the last but one, and I had to clear the last; then four strides out he made up his mind he was going to hit it.

'He had got up-tight outside. It was just before the closing ceremony and all the flags were fluttering, and he just threw himself completely the wrong way around. He was just that sort of horse. He had jumped a magic round in the morning for four faults, but had got himself so excited and tense in the afternoon that there was no way he could do it, and he just took off at the last two jumps and it cost us a bronze medal. Imagine how sick I was.

'I always said that if there was a hole in the ground and you took him out exercising, he would fall in it going out and fall in the same hole coming back.'

St James

If horses such as Heatwave and Feedback can be placed reliably in the second division, not all horses who are sold on are less brilliant. David bought a little six-year-old chestnut gelding on his record, having tried him once in an indoor school. 'It was only after I bought him that a couple of people said "Have you seen the way he drops one leg down?" I hadn't, but if a horse leaves a leg down when he's jumping a vertical, it's nearly a guaranteed way of having a bad fall, and I must say, if I went to try a horse and noticed him doing it, I don't think I would buy him. So whenever I jumped this horse at home, I never allowed him the opportunity to put a leg down. I'd put a V in front of the fence to give him a chance to get his front end up, and he might have left a leg down with me perhaps once, up to the time we sold him. We called him Harris Home Care and I won nearly £40,000 on him, but I always felt a bit too big on him.'

The horse in question was renamed St James by his new owner and the ride went to Nick Skelton, for whom he was immensely successful and almost unbeatable against the clock. He did once or twice succumb to the habit of dropping a leg, in particular giving Nick a crashing fall jumping a combination in the King's Cup at White City. However, he won many prestigious competitions, including the King's Cup. 'He had a heart of gold and a lot of ability,' says David. 'In particular he had a very rare ability when he was in the air, that if he was in trouble, he could go again.'

Prolific winner Harris Home Care (later St James) at Arena North.

Sportsman

If there was one horse, above all others, whom David would never have sold or passed on, it was Sportsman. Throughout the 1970s two horses, Sportsman and Philco, kept David's name in the international limelight. 'I was very lucky to have them both at the same time, and they were probably two of the best ten horses in the world at the time. I could go to Wembley and it didn't matter which one I pulled out at night, because either one could go and win. It was a lovely feeling to have that option.'

Sportsman was one of those horses destined for greatness from the very beginning. Firstly, like so many of the good ones, he came from Frank Kernan's yard in Ireland; secondly, his impression on David was immediate and convincing; thirdly, his impression on the rest of the world was the same.

'I bought him as a four-year-old. I was standing at Frank Kernan's kitchen window at breakfast time, looking out at the paddock outside, and I saw this horse just jump this fence – talk about bells ringing and lights flashing!'

The star in the making did not shine as a novice, however, and was to be dogged all his life by a series of soundness problems. 'I produced him right through the grades,' remembers David. He was probably the most intelligent horse I have ever had, and so understanding. He used to walk the ring and could really weigh up the jumps before you started. He had a nice name which suited him, and everyone who knew anything about horses knew he was going to be a great horse.

'In his third year they wanted him on the team at Hickstead and I wouldn't allow it, because I said the fences would be too big there and they could have him at Dublin instead. So we duly went to Dublin for the Aga Khan trophy in 1972, and they built the biggest course, probably, that Dublin has ever seen. All the great nations were there, getting ready for the Olympic Games, and there I am with my seven-year-old novice horse in his first Nations Cup.

'Well, I jumped and he had two rounds of four faults. He jumped all the problem fences and in fact he was the second best horse in the whole competition, beaten only by the top German mare, Simona. I was asked to take him to the Olympics that year, but I wouldn't because he wasn't ready for it.'

As mentioned earlier (pages 36-7), being faced with such a huge course so early in his career gave the talented young horse a considerable mental setback, from which he did not recover for twelve months. Such an experience would have marked the end of the career of many a potential star, but it is a tribute to David's understanding of the situation and patience in dealing with it that he did overcome it, and that Sportsman went on to fulfil his destiny.

'For twelve months I couldn't put any pressure on him in the ring. He was a blood horse and got terribly worried about things. He had a period after Dublin of having seventeen seconds without winning a class, but then we broke the mould at Surrey County. There were only two clear rounds in the class – Alan Oliver and myself. Alan went first in the jump-off and had sixteen faults; I went in and had twelve. What a way to break it! He never had the chance to win another competition as easily as that.

'After that, he went on and on. We went to the Lancia final four years out of five. The format was a one-round speed class and a three-round jump-off, and in four years he jumped seventeen clear rounds out of seventeen. One year I was even on points with Derek Ricketts for the car; we went into a special jump-off and Derek had one down and I beat him.

'Sportsman won the Grand Prix at Dublin two years running. There was a double in the middle of the ring, probably the biggest I've ever jumped, with a vertical in and an oxer out. They put it up for all three rounds and the third time he jumped it better than either of the first two. He would try his heart out.'

Sportsman also won David his third King George V Cup, a Grand Prix at Olympia,

National Championships, and World Cup Qualifiers at Birmingham and Amsterdam. He competed in the World Championships, finishing fifth, and in a World Cup Final. Sadly, however, he was never free of his soundness problems and although his career spanned eight years at the highest level, after he retired they returned to trouble him.

'His tendon actually gave way in the end. We kept him going for six or seven weeks because I couldn't face the inevitable, but he couldn't come out of his stable and he was never going to get better.

'So I went away for four days.' Clearly the

The unforgettable Sportsman: he and David made a strong team in the mid-seventies, and David remembers the horse with great affection.

memory still hurts, but David continues.

'My vet, John McEwen [the show-jumpers' team vet] had had such a lot to do with him, keeping him sound over the years, and the horse had such a lovely character, that he asked me if his partner could put him down and not himself. He said if I wanted him to, he would do it – but it goes to show that there is a heart in these vets!

'I really got more attached to Sportsman than to anything else . . .'

Queensway's Big Q.

Queensway's Big Q

The back-up horse to Sportsman and Philco was Queensway's Big Q, the impressive grey from Germany. 'He was only about 16hh but he looked 17hh in the way he went. He had a high head carriage.'

Big Q stayed with David for three years and won many good classes, including helping to take team gold at the 1979 European Championships in Rotterdam; but the partnership was never completely compatible. 'He always jumped down the right-hand wing of a jump – it was murder! But he was honest, a little bit ambitious, but a terrific athlete over a fence.

'He wasn't easy to ride and I don't think we were totally suited to each other. It was just that he was so good that we got away with it.'

Eventually David decided to part company with him, and Big Q went initially back to Germany, to Paul Schockemöhle, and then on to a new career in America.

Mr Ross

Into the gap, from Switzerland, came Mr Ross – and the fifth King George V Gold Cup, in 1981. Mr Ross was quite the opposite in type to Big Q: 'He was 17hh, but short-coupled, and although not an extravagant jumper he was very fast against the clock.'

For several years he was a top money-winner, with the King's Cup, Leading Jumper of the Year, Victor Ludorum and the Everest Championship at Park Farm to his credit. Often he didn't want to collect his prize: 'If he had won the class, he would stand perfectly still and have his rosette and when the time came he would canter off, a bit sharply, but not really a problem. If he was fifth or sixth, he would stand and get his rosette until the winner moved off and then he was the most awkward animal you've ever come across. He'd run backwards, spin round and completely flip his mind.

'What I found out later was that one day in a parade in Toronto, he had looked around and seen a bull behind him! He never got over it.'

When Mr Ross retired he went to the girl groom who had looked after him, and when she went to America, to some other friends. 'But he was always mine, and when they no longer wanted him he came back, until finally he had to be put down.'

Philco

There is always room for David's retired horses at Mount Ballan, not least for the grey Philco, always a favourite with show-jumping fans and whose name appears in the top echelons of the record books from 1976 to 1982. 'The Arrogant Yankee, is what we called him. It was his attitude. He had the reputation of being the most expensive green horse ever sold from America. We went there looking for a top-class Grand Prix horse and we came back with him. I will never forget it.

'His first show was at Badminton and I registered him as a Grade B horse with £120, as that is what I thought he had won. He went in an A and B class, with a decent course around 4ft 6in to 4ft 9in and a jump-off of 5ft to 5ft 3in, and he jumped two clear rounds.

'Everybody turned up to see our new grey horse – nobody had been to America to buy a horse before – and he finished about fourth. It

148

was a beautiful day, absolutely perfect ground. Trevor Banks said "I wish I owned him and you had one better", which I thought was a lovely thing to say.

'I produced him that year quietly. In fact I didn't ride him against the clock for about three years. He wasn't a prolific winner in novice classes and I think that was his saving grace, as he would have got too quick too fast. He was an ex-racehorse, and it was only years later that I found out that when we bought him he had actually only won twelve dollars show jumping!

'If I had known that at the time, I would probably have tried to win the Foxhunter competition on him and it would have been the worst thing I could have done. I think the fact that he missed all those small classes – going like the clappers against the clock – was the making of him. He won nearly all his money in Grand Prix and at top class shows.'

More than ten years on, at twenty-eight years old, Philco is still enjoying his retirement. 'He lives the life of O'Reilly. He goes out when it's fine; when it's raining he doesn't want to go out. We found out that when he was resting, his heart could miss several beats; it was perfectly normal when he was in work, but it wasn't worth taking the risk of jumping him, so that's when we retired him. Over the years he had won about £180,000, which in those days was a lot of money.'

In conclusion

This roundup of the horses which have shared David's fame, plus the recently retired Phoenix Park; fast-against-the-clock Feedback; Countryman, who is so reminiscent of Sportsman; and Lannegan who is like no one but himself, brings us right up to date. Also the good young horse Showman is waiting in the wings – no doubt with others whose names have yet to be recorded, since David says 'Nobody has ever beaten Father Time yet, but my horses will still carry me and my nerve will still take me down to the big fence.'

It also brings us to the close of this book; which we hope has succeeded in giving some insight into the skill, the methods and the sympathetic horsemanship of a great show-jumping rider; also his pragmatic realism, his magical performances and not least, his school of philosophical thought – or to put it another way, 'feel': which, without a doubt, is the legacy of David Broome to the show jumpers of the future.

INDEX

Page references in *italic* indicate illustrations